Community of Creativity

A Century of MacDowell Colony Artists

Organized by
P. Andrew Spahr

with a Foreword by
William Nathaniel Banks

and Essays by
Robert Storr
Tom Wolf

The Currier Gallery of Art • Manchester • New Hampshire

This book has been published in conjunction with the exhibition *Community of Creativity: A Century of MacDowell Colony Artists*, organized by The Currier Gallery of Art with leadership support from Chubb Life, a member of the Chubb Group of Insurance Companies. Additional funding for the exhibition has been generously provided by The DuBose and Dorothy Heyward Memorial Fund and The Brown Foundation, Inc.

Exhibition Tour

The Currier Gallery of Art
Manchester, New Hampshire
September 13 – December 2, 1996

Wichita Art Museum
Wichita, Kansas
April 20 – June 15, 1997

Photograph Credits
Harry Bartlett: 84; William H. Bengtson: 70; Frank Cordelle: 83; Dennis Cowley: 73; Jean Crossman: 91; Dean Powell Photography: 97; D. James Dee: 62, 68; Liz Deschenes: 95; Bill Finney: 36, 37, 61, 76, 81; Jim Frank: 65, 89; Carole Gallagher: cover and 44; Gamma One Conversions: 87; Andrew Gillis, Cascadilla Photography: 94; Ray Graham: 85; Mark Gulezian, Quicksilver Photographers: 64; E. Huntington Huggins, courtesy of the MacDowell Colony: 18; Peter Jacobs: 92; Courtesy of Janet Marqusee Fine Arts: 52; Clemens Kalischer, courtesy of the MacDowell Colony: 14; Courtesy of Kennedy Galleries Inc., New York: 86; Basil Langton, courtesy of the MacDowell Colony: 16; Courtesy of the MacDowell Colony: 2, 20, 41; Edward MacDowell, courtesy of the MacDowell Colony: 43; Gary Mamay: 49; Courtesy of Marlborough Gallery, Inc.: 90; All Rights Reserved, The Metropolitan Museum of Art: 56, 60, 66, 77, 82; © Joanna Eldredge Morissey: 12; Muldoon Studio: 54; 1996 © The Museum of Modern Art, New York: 93; Courtesy of the National Museum of American Art: 71; Courtesy of The National Museum of Women in the Arts: 80; Courtesy of the New-York Historical Society: 24; Bernice B. Perry, courtesy of the MacDowell Colony: 15, 22, 30; George Potanovic, Jr., Sun Studios: 72; Adam Reich: 96; Courtesy of Salander-O'Reilly Galleries: 50; Manu Sassoonian: 46; Steven Sloman, produced and published by Tyler Graphics Ltd. © John Newman / Tyler Graphics Ltd. 1992: 78; Craig Smith: 74; Steven Tucker: 59; Jakrarat "Oi" Veerasarn: 48; Carey A. Walbridge, Peterborough, NH, courtesy of the MacDowell Colony: 26; Nicholas Walster: 69; Sarah Wells: 67, 88; © 1996 Whitney Museum of American Art, Geoffrey Clements: 53, 55, 57; Chee-Heng Yeong: 51.

Artists' Statements
Avery: collection of the MacDowell Colony Archives, Peterborough, New Hampshire; Gillespie: from a statement written to Nancy Englander, Resident Manager, in response to request, collection of the MacDowell Colony Archives, Peterborough, New Hampshire; Perry: Library of Congress, Manuscript Division, MacDowell Colony Papers.

Distributed by University Press of New England
Hanover and London

Library of Congress Cataloguing-in-Publication data
Spahr, P. Andrew
Community of Creativity: *A Century of MacDowell Colony Artists*/essays by Tom Wolf, Robert Storr; catalogue by P. Andrew Spahr.
Catalogue of an exhibition to be held at The Currier Gallery of Art, Manchester, New Hampshire beginning September 13, 1996, and at other museums.
Includes listing of visual artists' residencies at MacDowell Colony.
ISBN 0-929710-19-3
1. 96-85645

Publication Coordinator: Michele Marcantonio
Design and typography: Gilbert Design Associates, Inc.
Editor: Evelyn Rosenthal
Printed in United States of America

Cover Photograph: Carole Gallagher
Frontispiece: Alexander Studio, courtesy of the MacDowell Colony

Contents

Lenders to the Exhibition

ACA Galleries, New York/Munich
Candida Alvarez
Benny Andrews
Kristine Yuki Aono
William Nathaniel Banks
Christina Bertoni
Ralph T. Cantin
The Currier Gallery of Art, Manchester, New Hampshire
Simon Dinnerstein
Michael David Echols
Janet Fish
Louise Fishman
Patricia Tobacco Forrester
Jessica Fredericks Gallery, New York
Dr. and Mrs. William Fritz
Grey Art Gallery & Study Center, New York University Art Collection
June Kelly Gallery Inc., New York
Kennedy Galleries Inc., New York
Phyllis Kind Gallery, New York/Chicago
Harry E. Leigh
Glenn Ligon
Marlborough Gallery, Inc., New York
Jason McCoy, Inc., New York
The Metropolitan Museum of Art, New York
Robert Miller Gallery, New York
The Montclair Art Museum, New Jersey
Museum of Art, Rhode Island School of Design, Providence
The Museum of Modern Art, New York
National Museum of American Art, Smithsonian Institution, Washington, D.C.
The National Museum of Women in the Arts, Washington, D.C.
Neuberger Museum of Art, Purchase College, State University of New York
The Newark Museum, New Jersey
Patricia and Donald Oresman
Phoenix Art Museum, Arizona
Mrs. Elizabeth D. Prestopino
Max Protetch Gallery, New York
Rose Art Museum, Brandeis University, Waltham, Massachusetts
Salander-O'Reilly Galleries, New York
Tyler Graphics Ltd., Mount Kisco, New York
University Gallery, University of Massachusetts at Amherst
Wendell Street Gallery, Cambridge, Massachusetts
Whitney Museum of American Art, New York
Wichita Art Museum, Kansas
Wright Gallery, New York
Andre Zarre Gallery, New York
and several private collections

Preface

THIS CATALOGUE and the exhibition it accompanies celebrate one of the great resources of New Hampshire, the MacDowell Colony in Peterborough. Though MacDowell is the oldest and largest artists' retreat in America, it is not well known to the public at large precisely because it strives to offer a protected nurturing environment away from the workaday world, where artists can concentrate on creative endeavors.

The Currier Gallery of Art is proud to be part of a statewide collaboration of more than fifty cultural organizations and a distinguished group of companies, foundations, state agencies, and individuals who have joined together to celebrate the centennial of the beginnings of the MacDowell Colony. As a result, a rich array of exhibitions, concerts, readings, and performances – all celebrating the work of MacDowell fellows – are being presented in 1996 in virtually every corner of New Hampshire.

The kernel from which this collaboration has flourished was planted in 1993 by a steering committee comprised of John F. Swope, Vice President of the Currier Gallery of Art and, at that time, President of Chubb Life; Linda Frawley, Assistant Vice President of Government and Public Affairs of Chubb Life; Thomas P. Putnam, Chief Executive Officer of Markem Corporation and President of the MacDowell Colony; Mary Carswell, Executive Director of the MacDowell Colony; William N. Banks, a MacDowell Trustee and former fellow; and my predecessor, Marilyn F. Hoffman. Theresa M. Stone, President and Chief Executive Officer of Chubb Life, has enthusiastically supported this endeavor since her arrival in New Hampshire.

This catalogue and exhibition are the most comprehensive to date to document the MacDowell experience for visual artists. Early on in the development of the exhibition an advisory committee – William N. Banks; Ned Rifkin, Director, High Museum of Art, Atlanta; William S. Lieberman, Jacques and Natasha Gelman Chairman of 20th-Century Art, The Metropolitan Museum of Art; Thomas Sokolowski, Director, Andy Warhol Museum, Pittsburgh; Varujan Boghosian, artist; Joan Washburn, Washburn Gallery, New York; Ellen Simak, Curator, Hunter Museum of Art, Chattanooga; Robert Storr, Curator of Painting and Sculpture, The Museum of Modern Art, New York; Lowery S. Sims, Curator, 20th Century Art, The Metropolitan Museum of Art; Margo Machida, Independent Curator and Visiting Professor in Art History at Brandeis University; and Marilyn F. Hoffman – helped with the awesome task of suggesting some fifty visual artists to be included in the exhibition out of a possible thirteen hundred who have resided at MacDowell. The final selection has been made by Andrew Spahr, Curator of the Currier Gallery of Art. Not only has he shaped a beautiful exhibition, but he has also successfully brought together a remarkably diverse group of works which reflects the wide embrace of the colony itself. Mr. Spahr, with Assistant Curator Michele Marcantonio, has overseen every detail of organizing the show and producing this handsome publication. Lisa Weber Greenberg, Curator of Exhibitions at the Art Complex Museum, Duxbury, Massachusetts, saw the project through its early phases of development and research. David Macy, Resident Manager of the MacDowell Colony, and his colleague Elizabeth Michael, Communication Coordinator, have provided invaluable information on the colony and its fellows.

More than forty lenders – museums, galleries, artists, and private collectors – have generously parted with paintings and sculptures to make this exhibition possible. Almost every department within the Currier has contributed to the success of the project. I extend thanks to Kathy Ritter, Librarian; Karen Papineau, Registrar; Hetty Startup, Zimmerman House Site Administrator; Britt Steen Zuñiga, Education Programs Coordinator; Mary Christo, Education Administrator; Stephanie B. Neal and Dennett M. Page, Development Department; Kathleen N. Williams, Public Relations and Marketing Manager; and Alan Grimard, Ron Sklutas, Bernard Lord, and Robert Desrocher of Buildings and Grounds. Susan L. Leidy, Deputy Director, has contributed to the MacDowell project in a variety of substantive ways, as the first coordinator of the New Hampshire MacDowell Celebration and as a member of the Currier staff. Joe Gilbert and Gilbert Design Associates have created a handsome catalogue design, and Evelyn Rosenthal has served as the publication editor. I would also like to recognize Inez McDermott for her valuable suggestions on the project. They all have our deep appreciation and thanks.

The catalogue offers fresh insights into the founding of the colony as well as the impact of its artistic legacy through the thoughtful, intelligent essays of Tom Wolf, Associate Professor of Art History, Bard College, and of Robert Storr. The catalogue has been greatly enriched with statements by five artists and former MacDowell fellows, Milton Avery, Gregory Gillespie, Susan Hambleton, Carol Hepper, and Lilla Cabot Perry, who describe the impact of their residencies.

None of this would have been possible without the generous support of many partners. We are deeply grateful to Chubb Life, not only for its leadership support of the exhibition and catalogue but for its role in developing the statewide MacDowell celebration. Throughout the many phases of this project, Chubb Life has been an encouraging and generous force. Additional funding was provided by The DuBose and Dorothy Heyward Memorial Fund and The Brown Foundation, Inc. The Currier is also grateful to Monadnock Paper Mills, Inc., of Bennington, New Hampshire for their support.

Together with all those who have supported this project, the Currier is proud to introduce the MacDowell experience to a national audience. We thank our colleagues at the Wichita Art Museum in Wichita, Kansas, who are also presenting this show.

But most of all we thank Edward and Marian MacDowell, whose vision and devotion to the creative spirit inspired this celebration of the MacDowell Colony, their lasting contribution to the artistic life of the nation.

Susan Strickler
Director
The Currier Gallery of Art

Acknowledgments

THE REMARKABLE EXPERIMENT begun in Peterborough, New Hampshire, by Edward and Marian MacDowell is alive today in the creativity of the current colony residents and in the remarkable visual legacy displayed in this centennial exhibition. The Currier Gallery of Art has drawn from its own and other distinguished public and private collections to create *Community of Creativity: A Century of MacDowell Colony Artists.*

As founder of the New Hampshire celebration of the one hundredth anniversary of the MacDowell Colony, Chubb is pleased to sponsor an enduring chronicle of the colony's contribution to the visual arts through this exhibition and catalogue. We applaud the commitment and vision of the colony and the depth and breadth of the artistry it fosters.

THERESA M. STONE
President & Chief Executive Officer
Chubb Life – A Member of the Chubb Group of Insurance Companies

THE MACDOWELL COLONY has been privileged to be part of New Hampshire's celebration of works of art produced by colony fellows in the past hundred years. First thanks must go to Linda Frawley, whose question to me, "Has MacDowell ever been honored by this state?" started the whole rich conversation; to John F. Swope, then President of Chubb Life, who lent his intelligence, personal conviction, and corporate leadership; to Chubb Life's President and Chief Executive Officer, Theresa M. Stone, John's successor, who brought her own enthusiasm to the project; to each of the other members of the steering committee: William N. Banks, a MacDowell Trustee and former fellow; Marilyn F. Hoffman, former Director of the Currier Gallery of Art, and her successor, Susan Strickler; and Thomas P. Putnam, Chief Executive Officer of Markem Corporation and President of the MacDowell Colony, who has been consistently wise and determined and who has helped the celebration live up to all our hopes and expectations. Without the fine, good-humored guidance and hard work of both of our coordinators, first Susan Leidy and then Andrea Silver, we would still be dreaming of a New Hampshire MacDowell Celebration. Congratulations and thank you to Andrew Spahr, Curator, and all those at the Currier Gallery of Art who have worked to make *Community of Creativity: A Century of MacDowell Colony Artists* a wonderful exhibition. And may the friendships and collaborations that have grown during the planning of the celebration continue to flourish.

MARY CARSWELL
Executive Director
The MacDowell Colony

Foreword

WILLIAM NATHANIEL BANKS

AS A MEMBER of the board of the MacDowell Colony for thirty years, and as a former colonist, I am a wholehearted celebrant of this national treasure. Grateful as I am for our splendid museums, libraries, and concert halls, which preserve the masterworks of the past, I fervently believe that unless we produce abundant *new* art – art that is vital, trenchant, and relevant to our time and place – we cannot claim to be a civilized nation. The composer Edward MacDowell and his wife Marian, who bought a farmhouse and a tract of woodland in Peterborough, New Hampshire, in 1896, conceived the MacDowell Colony as an incubator of the creative arts.

After MacDowell's death in 1908 the indomitable Marian built the colony studio by studio, realizing their dream. She battled blizzards, the flooding of the Contoocook River, a hurricane, and a devastating fire. She faced incessant fiscal crises. To raise money she repeatedly crisscrossed the country, performing MacDowell's piano pieces in concert and establishing colony support clubs in places as remote as El Paso and Oklahoma City. Her mission was "to maintain ... at the home of Edward MacDowell, a colony where working conditions most favorable to the production of enduring works of imagination, shall be provided for creative artists." Today there are thirty-two studios strategically scattered over 450 acres of pine groves and meadows with glimpses of Mount Monadnock in the distance.

Why *is* the MacDowell formula so wonderfully favorable to creativity? The arcadian setting and the isolation and womblike security of each studio, where lunch is delivered on the doorstep in a picnic basket, insure days of unbroken solitude. Convivial evenings in Colony Hall provide the opportunity for rousing encounters among the artists that sometimes lead to collaboration and, occasionally, to romance and marriage.

Not to be discounted is the effect of the benign ghosts that haunt the studios. Composer David Diamond insists that on a July evening in 1935 he actually saw, seated at the piano in the Sprague-Smith studio, the bronze-haired poet Elinor Wylie, a glamorous femme fatale who had worked at MacDowell in the early twenties and had died in 1928. The spirit of Aaron Copland is thought to linger in his favorite studio, Chapman, where he wrote *Appalachian Spring*. A painter might sense the aura of Milton Avery in the space where, on several visits to the colony, he refined his brilliant pictorial shorthand; and a writer occupying the Veltin studio would surely be aware that it was there Thornton Wilder enlivened *Our Town* with his observations of Peterborough folkways. These august phantoms, instead of being scary or intimidating, are in fact inspiring, and they contribute to the magic of MacDowell.

But perhaps magic should not, probably cannot, be analyzed. Suffice it to say, the MacDowell formula is marvelously effective. It seems the waves of creative energy emanating from the studios and vibrating in the clear upland air do stimulate the artists to work at the top of their form, for most of them will tell you they have done more – and often better – work at the colony than they have ever done elsewhere.

At a time when the attitude in Washington toward artistic pursuits is frequently adversarial, it is more important than ever for the MacDowell Colony, and other artists' colonies that have followed its lead, to provide ideal working conditions for the men and women who have made a lifetime commitment to the arts. It is reassuring to know that every morning of the year professional artists, after breakfasting at Colony Hall, are walking down the shady lanes to their studios where, in the awful stillness, they will create some of the new artworks without which we would become a soulless people.

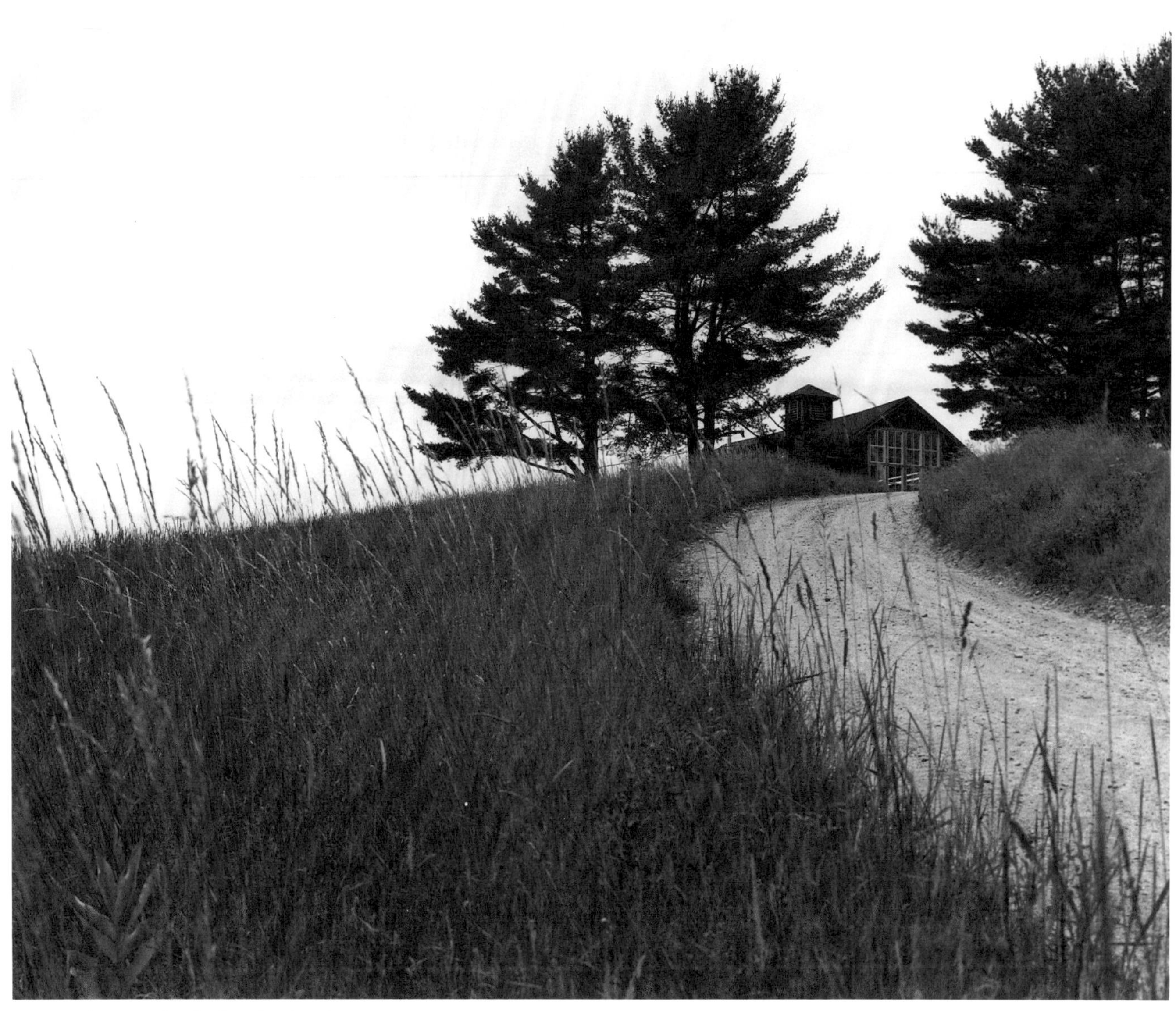

FIG. 1. The Barn Studio for visual artists

A Gift of Time and Solitude

P. Andrew Spahr

> *"Whatever influences the art of a country, influences in the most intimate sense its civilization, and certainly few people are aware that MacDowell's plan, now proved practical beyond question, is one of national importance."*
>
> —Mary Mears
> *MacDowell colonist*, 1909[1]

As we go about our busy lives in the complex and distracting late twentieth century with multiple commitments to career, family, and community, we often find ourselves longing for peace and solitude. We seek a retreat not just for relaxation, but for work, to meet impending deadlines or to address projects long put aside. Imagine having a place to work that is yours alone for several weeks, with no telephone or television and no interruptions. That place would be one of the private, secluded studios at the MacDowell Colony. An opportunity to work creatively in a highly focused way is what visual artists, writers, poets, architects, and composers seek out and find at MacDowell. As MacDowell Fellows they leave the world behind for one or two months and accept the gift of solitude and time that the colony provides.

The MacDowell Colony was established to allow artists of various disciplines to work free from distraction while at the same time engaging in thoughtful dialogue with one another. Founded in 1907 by the prominent American composer Edward MacDowell and his wife Marian, the MacDowell Colony sits on 450 acres of hilly, forested land in the small town of Peterborough in the rural southwest corner of New Hampshire. The natural beauty of the setting is enhanced by views of nearby Mount Monadnock, the region's scenic highlight, which has inspired generations of artists and writers. The MacDowell grounds comprise thirty-two individual studios and associated support buildings. Linked by a network of lanes and paths, the studios are discreetly arranged about the colony, each one well distanced from its neighbors (fig. 1). This arrangement allows for the complete privacy of all colonists as they engage in their creative endeavors. Each studio has a distinctive architectural character and, although comfortable, is rustic and Spartan and offers little distraction from the work at hand. Wooden tablets hanging on the studio walls bear the signatures of their previous occupants (fig. 2). Following a long-standing tradition at MacDowell, a picnic basket lunch is delivered unobtrusively to each studio door, allowing for an uninterrupted work day. Colonists have access to studio

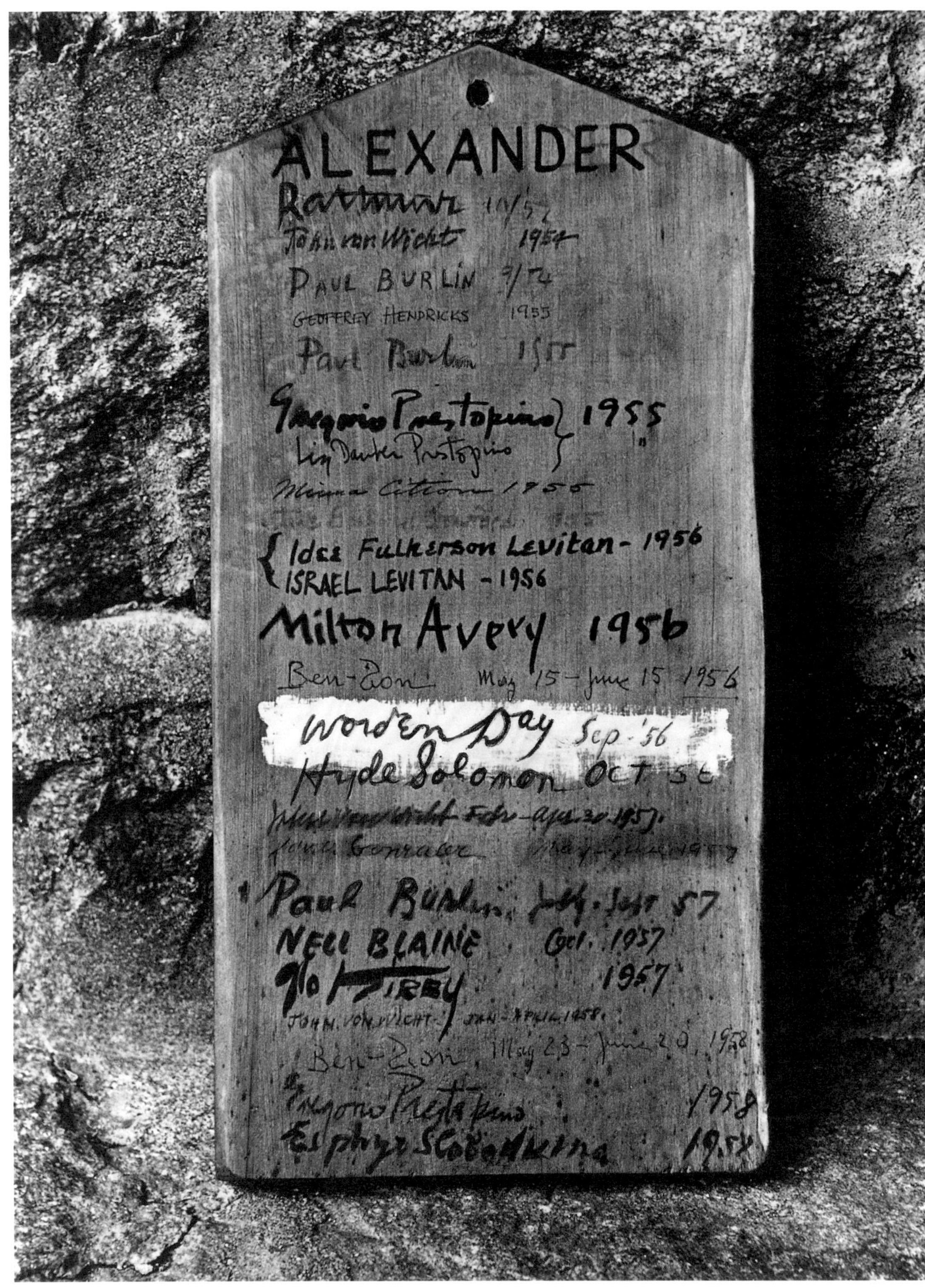

FIG. 2. One of the several Alexander Studio "tombstones" with signatures of resident artists

spaces day and night and can work according to their own schedules.

The colony's emphasis on individual creativity is tempered by a communal atmosphere. Colony Hall, a large barn renovated during the years 1913–25, serves as the hub of the community, with administrative offices and a dining room where fellows eat breakfast and dinner with their colleagues (fig. 3). Sleeping quarters are located in three buildings near Colony Hall. The campus also has a library with an extensive collection of writings and recorded music by past colonists. The library and Colony Hall serve as meeting places for planned presentations or impromptu gatherings where colonists may discuss their work and new ideas (fig. 4). It was Edward MacDowell's intention that the colony foster just such a dialogue, which often inspires collaboration between practitioners of the various arts.

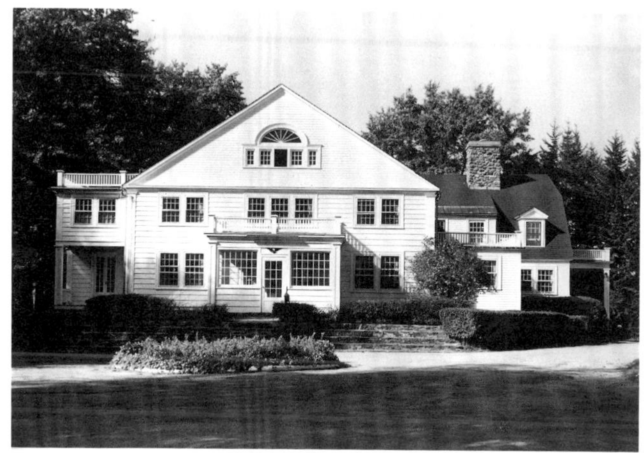

FIG. 3. Colony Hall

Since its inception the colony has shown a single-minded commitment to its founders' concept and has been providing the same important service to artists for nine decades. With its unique character, individual work studios, and historic buildings, the MacDowell Colony has long been recognized as an important contributor to the cultural life of the nation. In 1963 the colony was designated a National Historic Landmark by the U.S. Department of the Interior, and in 1966 it was entered on the National Register of Historic Places.

During this century, over forty-five hundred fellows have attended the MacDowell Colony, of which more than thirteen hundred have been visual artists working in a variety of media including painting, sculpture, printmaking, and photography. Ten of the thirty-two studios are specifically set up to accommodate visual artists by providing ample work space and northern light. Currently the colony is outfitting a full-scale sculpture studio with the necessary tools for working stone, wood, and metal, as well as facilities for handling large objects, thus making a MacDowell stay an even more attractive prospect for artists engaged in three-dimensional work.

"Talent is the sole criterion for acceptance to the MacDowell Colony," according to the application brochure. Each year the colony receives about 1,200 applications across all disciplines for the approximately 215 fellowships available throughout the year. Applicants for the visual arts fellowships are required to submit five slides, past exhibition information, and two letters of reference. The finalists are selected by a committee of five, including artists, critics, scholars, teachers, and curators, who seek out mature, established artists as well as promising younger talents.

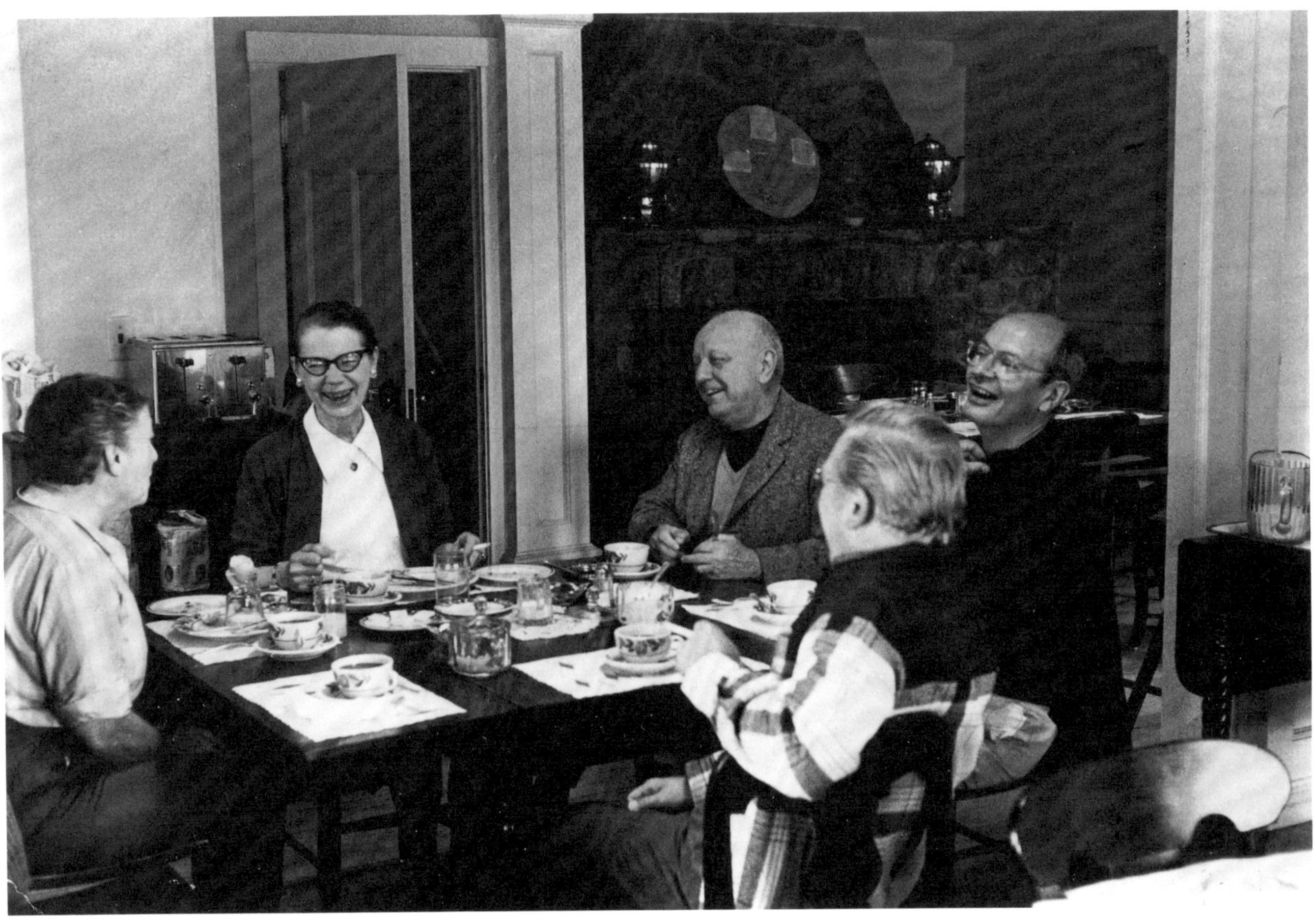

FIG. 4. Dining Room conversation, clockwise from left: Hortense Powdermaker, anthropologist; Louise Talma, composer; Virgil Thompson, composer; Hyde Solomon, painter; and Warren Benson, composer, 1963.

Often colonists return to MacDowell several times. However, a new application is required for each residence. While the great majority of colonists have come from the United States, fellows from abroad are becoming more common.

MacDowell's admission process has, from the very beginning, fostered the acceptance of a population of artists diverse in every way. Of particular note is the fact that since its first years of operation, at least in the visual arts, more women than men have worked at the colony. To allow for maximum accessibility, the modest residence fees paid by the colonists are voluntary, and the colony has recently introduced grant programs to cover travel expenses in cases of proven financial need.

This year marks the one hundredth anniversary of Marian and Edward MacDowell's purchase of their initial parcel of land in Peterborough. In the true spirit of Edward MacDowell's interdisciplinary approach to the arts, more than fifty cultural institutions in New Hampshire have joined together to develop a year-long celebration of the colony and its important and vibrant role in the nation's cultural life. The MacDowell Celebration includes musical and theatrical performances, poetry readings, and art and history exhibitions. The Currier Gallery of Art has contributed to the festivities by organizing this exhibition of selected work by artists who have attended the colony over the last nine decades. This is particularly fitting since in 1937 the Currier organized the only other museum-sponsored exhibition devoted to MacDowell artists.[2]

Community of Creativity: A Century of MacDowell Colony Artists is intended to show the great variety in subjects, styles, and aesthetic approaches of artists who have resided at the colony. However, no project with over thirteen hundred visual artists to choose from could hope to present a comprehensive picture of such creative multiplicity. From the 1906 portrait of Edward MacDowell (cat. no. 32) by the colony's first visual arts fellow Helen Farnsworth Mears, to recent works by young artists just beginning their careers, the diversity of artists included in this exhibition reflects the long-standing openness of the MacDowell Colony in choosing its fellows. Many works provide clues to the varied backgrounds of the colonists by exploring issues of personal and cultural identity. Through this exhibition the Currier has also sought to capture a sense of the look and feel of the MacDowell grounds and studios. A number of works depict views of rural New England and of the colony itself. In numerous cases the works were created during years that included a MacDowell residency, while many pieces actually originated or were completed during the artist's stay.

This catalogue presents new information on the history of the MacDowell Colony as well as several viewpoints on the MacDowell experience. In his essay Tom Wolf, Associate Professor of Art History at Bard College, discusses the colony's founding and its philosophical underpinnings in the MacDowell Club of New York City. Robert Storr, Curator of Painting and Sculpture at The Museum of Modern Art, New York, has contributed an essay that provides an important perspective on the artists included in the exhibition and their relationship to this century's aesthetic developments in the visual arts. In addition, several statements by artists offer firsthand accounts of the importance of the MacDowell experience in their lives and their artistic development.

The Currier Gallery of Art, which has long celebrated achievement in the arts, is pleased to have this opportunity to focus attention on the creative activity our state and its cultural institutions have helped to inspire. As artists look to new endeavors in the next century, the MacDowell Colony will continue to fulfill Edward and Marian MacDowell's legacy by providing the valuable gift of time and solitude to those who seek it.

NOTES

1. MacDowell Colony Archives, Peterborough, New Hampshire. In 1908 writer Mary Mears and her sister, the sculptor Helen Farnsworth Mears (cat. no. 32), became the first artists to attend the MacDowell Colony.

2. *Exhibition of Paintings, Sculpture, and Prints by Artists of the MacDowell Colony of Peterborough, NH*, The Currier Gallery of Art, 6 July – 26 September 1937. Another exhibition, *Seven Decades of MacDowell Artists* was held at the James Yu Gallery, New York, 24–28 October 1976.

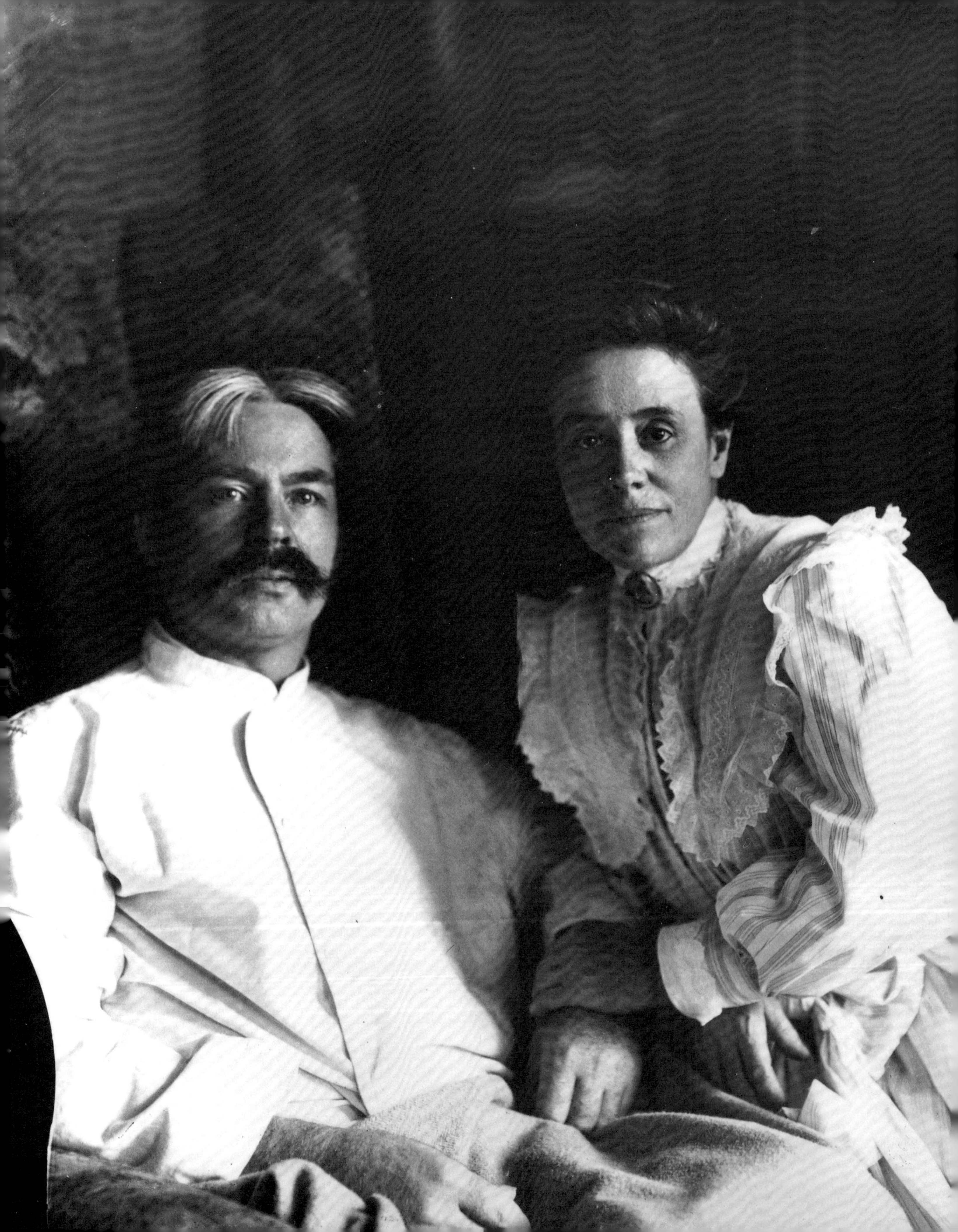

The Genesis of the MacDowell Colony

Tom Wolf

Celebrating the one hundredth anniversary of its beginnings, the MacDowell Colony looks back on a century of helping artists find invaluable time and peace in which to create their art. Although the colony has maintained a low profile over the decades, it is known to almost everyone in the visual, literary, and musical arts as a place artists can go to focus on their work with an unparalleled, almost unreal, absence of distractions. Despite its status as a household name in the arts, a century of single-minded dedication to the immediate needs of creative men and women has resulted in its remarkable early history being largely forgotten. But the story of its origins and its first years is a fascinating one, full of human drama, struggle, and accomplishment.

Edward MacDowell and the Idea of a Community of Artists

The colony was established in honor of Edward MacDowell, who played a key role in its conception and died a tragic death shortly after it began to function (fig. 1). Today the colony itself is better known than the man who inspired it, despite his immense fame during his lifetime, when he was esteemed as the first great American composer.

MacDowell was born in New York City in 1861; precociously talented, his skills included writing and drawing as well as music, which he went to study in Paris when he was fifteen. He continued his studies in Germany, and by age twenty he was head piano teacher at the Darmstadt Conservatory. The following year he met Franz Liszt, who encouraged the publication of his first piano concerto. His reputation as a composer and pianist rapidly grew in Europe and America, until his admirers urged him to return to the United States for the glory of his native country.

In 1884 MacDowell married the American-born Marian Nevins, who had studied piano with him in Germany, and who would become the moving force behind the MacDowell Colony after his death. In 1888 the couple settled in Boston where MacDowell continued composing and performing his works to great acclaim. In his *Indian Suite* the composer incorporated Native American melodies in a late romantic setting, asserting his Americanism in a way very popular with the concert-going public. It was first performed by the Boston Symphony Orchestra in New York in January 1896, and when Columbia University received funding to start a music department in the same year, MacDowell was the natural choice to head it. The hiring committee's opinion was that he was "the greatest musical genius America has produced."[1] Feeling great rapport with the university's president, Seth Low, he accepted the position, moved to New York, and threw himself into his new academic responsibilities with characteristic fervor. The handsome, intense composer was a great

Edward and Marian MacDowell, about 1906

success with the students, but his dedication to his job made finding time to compose difficult. After the MacDowells spent several summers renting accommodations in New Hampshire, Marian MacDowell found a large, secluded property in Peterborough which they bought in 1896 and which became their

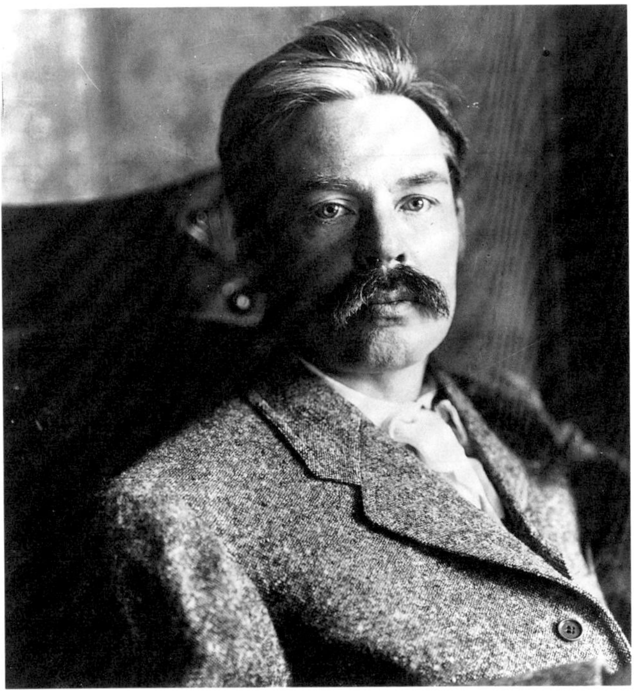

FIG. 1. Edward MacDowell, about 1906

summer retreat, where MacDowell composed his major late works.

When President Low left Columbia in 1901 to become mayor of New York he was replaced by Nicholas Murray Butler. MacDowell soon became frustrated with Butler's lack of enthusiasm for his ideas about the role of the arts in Columbia's curriculum. In early 1904 MacDowell submitted his letter of resignation to Columbia's trustees, along with a letter of criticism that set off a debate about education in the New York press. The argument was in part about the place of the arts in the university – MacDowell felt they were not taken seriously enough, and that they should be offered to the general undergraduate as well as to the specialist. He wanted several departments realigned to form a fine arts faculty: "I believe that music should never be treated alone, but only in conjunction with the fine arts, namely *belles lettres*, literature, painting, sculpture and architecture."[2] His opinion was rooted in his own talents – in his Paris days he was encouraged to pursue painting, and he frequently wrote poems to accompany his music, publishing a book of *Verses* in 1903 – and in Richard Wagner's influential theories on melding the diverse art forms. The idea became a central principle of the MacDowell Colony.

The academic debate was paralleled by a more personal one between MacDowell and Columbia. Butler published a letter stating that the two had parted amicably; MacDowell replied, stating that Butler's version was false, in a letter he sent to Columbia's trustees as well as to the *New York Times*. The trustees chastised MacDowell for sending a copy to the newspaper without first giving them time to respond, an action they termed "an offence against propriety."[3] While this seems like just another episode in the dispute, MacDowell's widow later wrote on the back of the trustees' letter, "It was this letter that seemed to break MacDowell's heart and crush his courage." He published a dignified response in one of the New York newspapers that carried the developments in this drama daily, but the entire affair greatly upset him. He began having difficulties sleeping, and he rapidly declined to where he could no longer compose, and soon could barely function. An accident in which he was struck by a hansom cab contributed to his deterioration. After years of precocious success, receiving great praise and making exhausting demands on himself, MacDowell had a mental breakdown from which he never recovered. According to his biographer, Lawrence Gilman,

> His mind became as that of a little child. He sat quietly, day after day, in a chair by a window, smiling patiently from time to time at those about him, turning the pages of a book of fairy tales that seemed to give him a definite pleasure, and greeting with a fugitive gleam of recognition certain of his more intimate friends.[4]

He declined rapidly and died on 23 January 1908, barely forty-seven years old.[5]

Today it is hard to imagine the adulation MacDowell inspired in the United States during his lifetime. Of course he had some detractors who questioned the greatness of his musical accomplishments, but they were in the minority. His good looks, his emotional, romantic compositions, his adoption of American themes (titling two sections of his *Woodland Sketches* "From an Indian Lodge," and "From Uncle Remus," for example), the fact that he was taken seriously by esteemed Europeans like Liszt and Edvard Grieg, plus his tragic demise, combined to make him a culture hero of major proportions. In the words of a writer for *Musical America*,

> The premature termination of Mr. MacDowell's career has long since taken its place among the greatest tragedies in the annals of music, not merely as regards art in this country, but in a universal sense, for his was the genius that cannot be limited by national barriers.[6]

Soon after his breakdown, friends and admirers of MacDowell had banded together to do something in his honor. The Mendelssohn Glee Club, a chorus of affluent young men which he had directed while he was at Columbia, started giving benefit concerts to raise funds to help him in his need, and also to carry out "his expressed ideas for the advancement of art in this country."[7] His reputation was so great, and sympathy for his plight so widespread, that an appeal for aid attracted such prominent citizens as former president Grover Cleveland, financier J. P. Morgan, and industrialist Andrew Carnegie.[8] Soon fundraising concerts were being planned all around the country, to help make MacDowell's property in New Hampshire a place "for students in all the arts, where quiet work and close companionship could be had."[9]

In his waning years MacDowell had come up with this idea with his wife. Shortly before his illness he was active as one of the founders of the American Academy of Arts and Letters, and as one of the first trustees of the American Academy in Rome, founded by his friend, the architect Charles McKim. Advising the Rome Academy led him to think about creating a comparable institution in the United States, where serious artists from various disciplines could work on their own projects in a creative community. Once he fell ill this idea remained with him, and when he became anxious about it his wife promised him that she would make it a reality.

Marian MacDowell's original 1896 purchase in Peterborough included close to sixty acres of woodland, with a farm that the MacDowells converted into their summer residence. There the composer still found himself subject to frequent interruptions and distractions, so his wife arranged to have a one-room cabin built in the woods, which became his composition studio and retreat (fig. 2). MacDowell's own need for solitude in order to work established the couple's idea that a creative artist periodically requires uninterrupted time alone, the concept that forms the rationale and determines the practice of the MacDowell Colony.

To fulfill her promise to her failing husband, Mrs. MacDowell soon took decisive action by deeding away the ownership of the Peterborough property to the MacDowell Association, which was established to receive and administer it. The association was comprised of Mrs. MacDowell plus representatives from two of the organizations that had recently supported

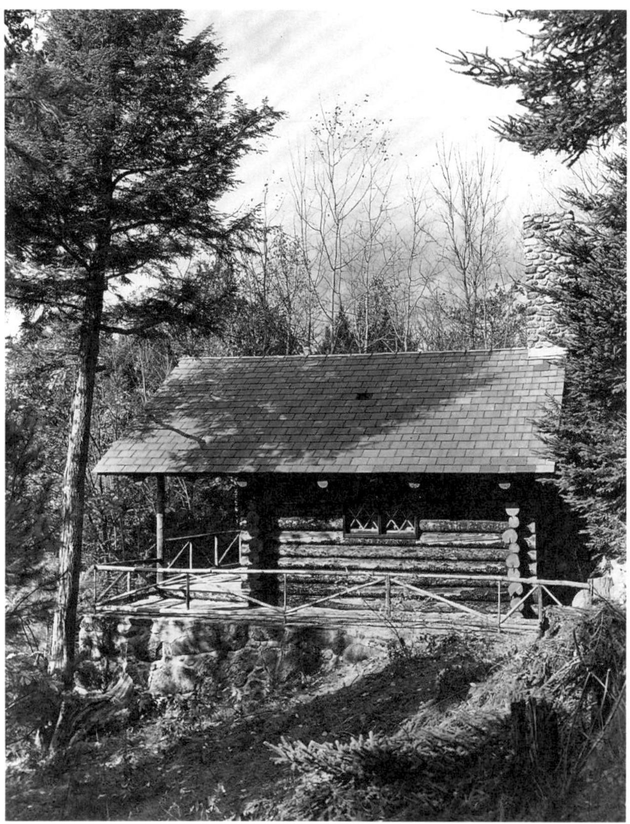

FIG. 2. Edward MacDowell's original studio constructed in 1899

MacDowell and his ideals, the Mendelssohn Glee Club, which had raised thirty thousand dollars in his name, and the MacDowell Club, an organization begun by his students, friends, and admirers.

IDEAS IN ACTION: THE MACDOWELL CLUB

Formed to further the composer's ideas about integrating the arts, the MacDowell Club came to play an extraordinarily dynamic role in the cultural life of New York City, a role that today has been mostly forgotten. The club showcased all the arts, with performances, recitals, exhibitions, and lectures. For example, Kurt Schindler formed the Schola Cantorum, a women's chorus, and soon it was accompanying the New York Philharmonic, conducted by Gustav Mahler.[10] The club's drama committee set up a system of previewing new plays and reviewing them for the general membership, which evolved into the Drama League of America, an organization active for decades in promoting theater in the United States. In addition, club members came up with innovative policies for the visual arts that made the organization a pivotal one in the art life of New York in the teens. In its first years the club honored its commitment to painting and sculpture by organizing exhibitions of works by established, well-respected figures such as Arthur B. Davies and Edwin Blashfield, but in the teens it developed a radical open exhibition policy that gave young artists like Stuart Davis, Edward Hopper, Yasuo Kuniyoshi, and scores of others some of their first opportunities to show their works in public.

When the club moved to new quarters at 108 West 55th Street in October 1911, the unprecedented exhibition policy was put into effect for the vaulted, seventy-five-foot-long gallery room (fig. 3). Any self-organized group of eight to twelve artists could exhibit there for the cost of invitations and opening expenses. The club took a welcoming but neutral position regarding these shows:

> Towards the groups the Club officiates as host. The Club stands neither for nor against the works exhibited. It offers its gallery as an open field for those who desire a public hearing....[11]

Hundreds of artists exhibited under the club's auspices over the next eight years. Many of the self-organized groups consisted mostly or entirely of women. Groups of Canadian artists showed there on several occasions, and the club hosted a show of the Japanese Artists Association. By creating an open, experimental venue for art exhibitions, the MacDowell Club enlivened the visual arts in a way that contrasted markedly with the restricted, juried shows held at the National Academy of Design.

Painter Robert Henri was the main moving force behind the club's innovative program. Although he was a member of the National Academy he opposed its juried exhibition policy, which had excluded several of his friends and artistic allies from Academy exhibitions. In 1908 he had reacted by organizing the famous exhibition of the Eight, held at the Macbeth Gallery, and followed it with the first Independent exhibition in 1910.[12] During these years Henri was a vocal and energetic proponent of liberal exhibition policies, and as a member of the MacDowell Club's Painting Committee he found a forum for his views.

Henri had a crucial ally in the painter John White Alexander, the club's president and a fellow member of its Painting Committee. In the New York art world of the early teens, Henri's portraits of urchins from the Lower East Side were the antithesis of Alexander's idealized women in flowing gowns. But Alexander was also open-minded and his own career had received a great boost in Paris in 1892 when his paintings were the sensation of the Salon du Champs-de-Mars, itself an alternative exhibition to the official Salon.[13] After he returned to the United States in 1901 Alexander became a celebrated and highly respected painter. He was a pallbearer at MacDowell's funeral and an active participant in MacDowell Club activities. In its early years he organized several evenings of tableaux vivants, where club members were costumed and posed to replicate old master paintings, holding their poses to the accompaniment of poems or musical compositions. A tradition popular in Europe in the nineteenth century, the tableau vivant also embodied the collaborative interaction of the arts that was MacDowell's ideal. One such program arranged by Alexander was presented at the Plaza Hotel on 8 November 1908. It included a pianist and a vocalist performing before scenes based on religious paintings, genre scenes, and, for the most part, portraits, by Van Eyck, Titian, Reynolds, and others. Another event combined MacDowell's *Sonata Eroica* with a reading from Tennyson and tableaux where Alexander posed his figures inside a large gold frame against a black velvet backdrop. He covered the front of the frame with black gauze and lit the scene with dim lights to create an intensely painterly effect.[14]

After the club moved in 1911, the new open exhibitions replaced these other events. In 1913 Alexander proudly announced that in its first season with the new program the club showed works by 102 artists, 32 of them women, in exhibitions seen by 9,500 viewers. He added that much of the American work in that year's famous Armory Show "was first shown on the walls of the MacDowell Club earlier this season."[15] While the club's unique exhibition policy was a corrective to the National Academy, it was a friendly rebellion because in fact the popular Alexander was not only president of the MacDowell Club, but simultaneously president of the Academy.

When Alexander died in 1915 his position as chairman of the MacDowell Club's Paintings Committee was filled by a close friend of Henri's, the painter George Bellows. Bellows strove to maintain the

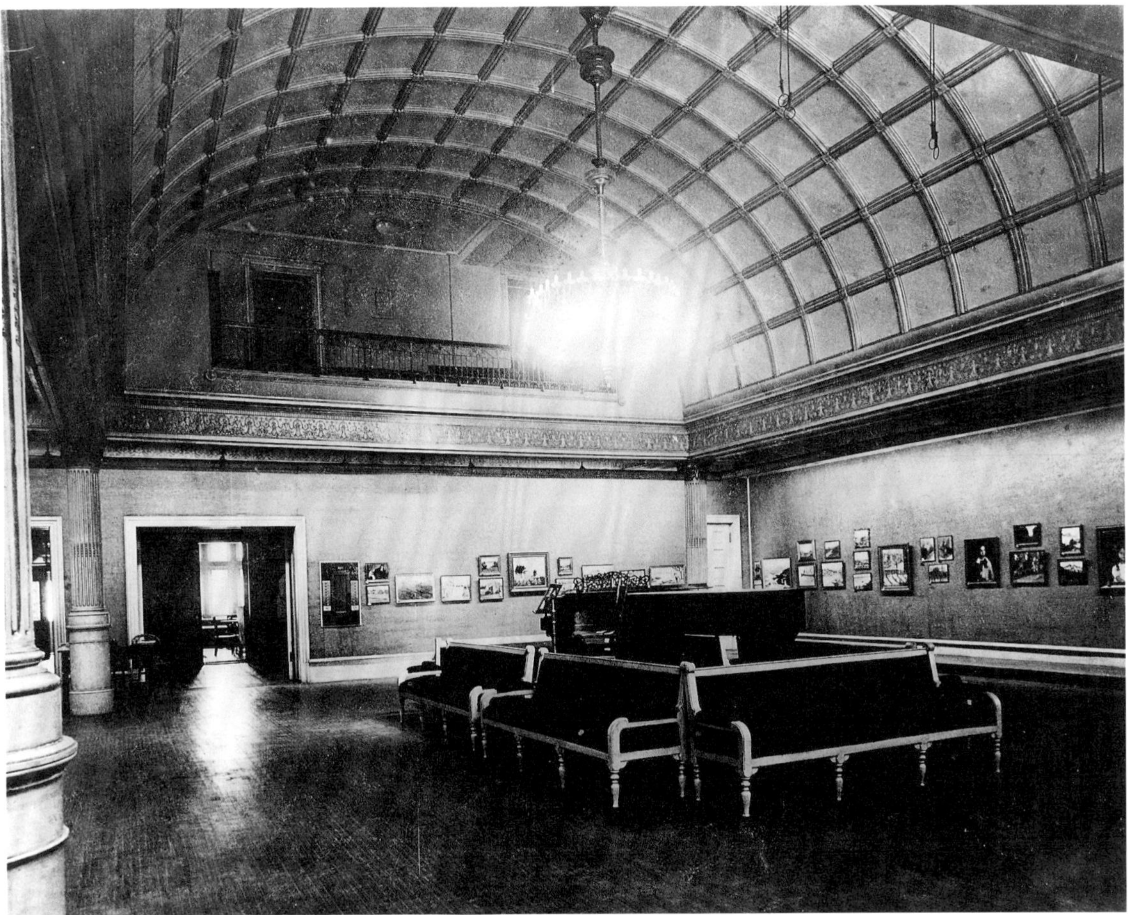

FIG. 3. The MacDowell Club (interior), New York

ambitious unjuried policy, but World War I brought a period of financial strain to the club, and increasingly there was a feeling that the exhibitions were declining in quality. Attendance was down and the shows were not reviewed regularly in the New York papers as they had been previously. Consequently, in 1919 it was decided, over Bellows's objections, to renovate the space and rent it out, putting an end after eight years to the extraordinary open policy that gave many of the most promising artists of the time a place to exhibit, and that was more accepting of diversity than most alternative exhibitions spaces are even today.

Although the exhibition program never recaptured its early vitality after its glory years in the teens, the MacDowell Club continued to function until World War II. Its art exhibitions were generally devoted to invited individuals or to groups of club members. Still the organization continued as an important forum for culture and the arts; for example, in November 1929 John Dewey lectured there, and a few days later a young Martha Graham performed her dance piece, *Immigrants*. But increasingly the schedule included commencement exercises for local schools and recitals by students of prominent piano teachers, events designed as much to generate income as to promote culture. As the Depression continued funds waned, and the trustees no longer came from the highest echelons of New York's cultural society. During World War II the American public was drawn to concerns other than the arts, and the club faced a steadily growing deficit. By 1942 the obstacles seemed too great, and it was decided to dissolve the club and sell its assets to cover its debts. Nevertheless, even in its final year the club hosted some events of remarkable interest along with its more routine offerings. The Hungarian composer Béla Bartók and his wife Ditta gave a concert of his pieces on twin pianos. The last art exhibition, also in 1942, was a mini-retrospective of works by Augustus Vincent Tack, an artist who still fascinates today with paintings that range from traditional portraits and religious paintings to innovative abstractions.

THE MOVING FORCE: MARIAN MACDOWELL

One sign of the club's diminishing vitality during its last years was the absence of the now elderly Mrs. MacDowell, the dynamic and dedicated force behind and symbolic locus of all the activities and organizations inspired by the composer. Marian Nevins MacDowell had in many ways as remarkable a life as her husband, whom she outlived by forty-eight years (fig. 4). Like him, she was born in New York City. A childhood accident forced her to spend much of her life on crutches, but her energy and positive personality seem to have made this impediment scarcely a handicap. "I flew around on my crutches almost as easily as though I were walking."[16] Her mother died when she was a child, leaving Marian, the oldest of three daughters, to become a helpmate to her father, a Wall Street lawyer. The many adult responsibilities Marian took on in the Nevins household established a pattern of nurturing behavior that was carried over to MacDowell, whom she married in 1884, the year of her father's death, and eventually to the colonists at Peterborough. She had studied piano with MacDowell for three years in Germany; when he proposed, she accepted on the condition that he stop working and they live off her inheritance for five years so that he could devote his time to composing. She put aside her own career as a pianist and dedicated herself exclusively to caring for her talented spouse. A miscarriage early in their marriage left her permanently unable to bear children; otherwise, she claimed, "My interests would have gone in the natural, human way instead of this other direction."[17] After her husband's death the MacDowell Club and particularly the colony became her primary interests. She resumed playing the piano after a ten-year hiatus, and began touring the United States giving performances of MacDowell's pieces. Over twenty-five years she gave around six hundred performances and earned more than one hundred thousand dollars, a major source of income for the colony.

The colony's beginnings date back to Edward MacDowell's final years, and the first two colonists came to Peterborough while he was still alive – Helen Farnsworth Mears, a talented young sculptor, and her writer sister, Mary. During MacDowell's last years his wife attempted to commission some of America's most successful artists, whom he knew personally, to make his portrait. The sculptor Augustus Saint-Gaudens wrote her that he was in poor health and overcommitted, but he could recommend a talented pupil and critique the results.[18] He apparently chose Helen Mears, a young artist whose work had been well received at the Columbian Exposition and who had subsequently studied with Saint-Gaudens and served as his assistant in Paris.[19] Her limpidly modeled relief depicts the composer seated in profile in his convalescent's chair, an open book on his lap as he stares into the distance (cat. no. 32). Mears traveled to Peterborough to work from her subject, and realized her portrait in a refined style that descends directly from her teacher, specifically from his famous portrait of Robert Louis Stevenson, who suffered from tuberculosis. Like Saint-Gaudens, Mears filled the empty space around the figure with text, in this case a passage of music from MacDowell's *Sonata Tragica* and a line from one of his poems, selected by the composer himself: "Night has fallen on a day of deeds."[20]

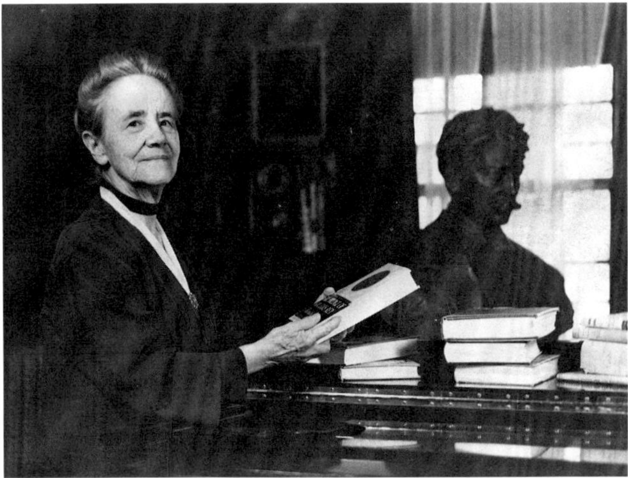

FIG. 4. Marian MacDowell, 1946

As a result of this commission the Mears sisters were invited to be the first artists to reside at the colony, which they did for part of each year from 1908 to 1911. Mrs. MacDowell, after recovering from the immediate effects of her husband's death, turned her energies towards the colony. She refused the moneys offered her by the various funds that had sprung up to help the ailing composer, but accepted them on behalf of the colony. She put the money to use immediately, buying land and buildings on the colony's perimeter to expand its space, erecting a prototype studio building, and establishing an endowment for the future. Soon she was planning activities to bring attention to the colony, beginning with an ambitious pageant in the summer of 1910. A three-day performance accompanied by music mostly composed by MacDowell, the pageant featured costumes designed by Miss Achsa Barlow, a pupil of the painter William Merritt Chase. A natural stage was cleared outdoors, framed by huge pines with a view of Mount Monadnock behind. A Peterborough choir organized by Mrs. MacDowell performed, along with musicians from Boston, some colonists, and scores of townspeople who wore period costumes to enact the history of the area. An introduction by the Muses was followed by scenes of Native American courtship, colonial times, and the Civil War. The precedent for this spectacular event was clearly the festivals organized by Wagner's widow at Bayreuth, which had a similar aim of combining the various arts.[21] Although it lost money, the pageant was a great critical success and the festivals were continued for the next three years, until interrupted by World War I. Concerts dominated the later festivals, sometimes accompanied by theatrical performance. The programs featured MacDowell's music along with compositions by contemporary Americans, often colonists who also conducted their own works. The first pageant had been the most elaborate, and it was repeated in 1919 at the request of the National Federation of Music Clubs.

During these years Mrs. MacDowell bought property bordering on colony land whenever it became available, raising funds however she could – mostly from her piano performances and from donations by sympathetic groups or individuals. The first colonists were all women because there was only one residential building besides Hillcrest, where Mrs. MacDowell lived. In 1911 she was able to purchase a nearby two-family house which was dubbed the Mannex and served as a place to house the male colonists who began to be invited that summer. The purchase of the Tenney Farm in 1912 added 184 acres, along with a farmhouse that was converted into another men's dormitory.[22] Meanwhile smaller buildings were remodeled into artists' studios, and new studios were financed by groups or by individuals such as John White Alexander's widow, who in 1916 donated a painting studio named after her husband.

The first colonists were simply acquaintances of the MacDowells. Then a committee was created to evaluate applicants, who needed letters of support from two established artists. Today prospective colonists apply with evidence of professional accomplishment and are selected by a committee of specialists in their field. Formerly Mrs. MacDowell sometimes made recommendations to the committee, just as she played a role in all aspects of the colony. As author Hermann Hagedorn wrote in 1947,

> For forty years, Mrs. MacDowell has been the Colony and the Colony has been Mrs. MacDowell; though she has always denied it, and managed to keep a straight face doing it. "I'm nobody," she would say. "My directors run the show. I just obey orders." This amiable fiction fooled nobody, least of all the directors....[23]

Early on she had started a full farm at the colony, managing a crew that worked to supply food for many of the colonists' meals, and by 1925 she had added a sawmill. A taxicab accident during a concert tour in 1923 had the unexpected result of improving her back condition, enabling her to walk without crutches. When a violent hurricane tore through the colony in 1938, destroying hundreds of trees and damaging many buildings, the eighty-two-year-old woman embarked on a concert tour to raise money and had the colony running again a year later. But by the mid-1940s, she was spending most of her time in the more soothing climate of Los Angeles, in the company of her companion, Nina Maude Richardson. Control of the colony gradually passed to the board of directors, and when Marian MacDowell died at age ninety-nine in 1957 a dedicated group of people was in place to ensure its continuation.

THE COLONY AT WORK

Artists are invited as individuals to the colony; families are not permitted, although a husband and wife can be admitted at the same time if both are artists, which has occurred often in the colony's history. The seclusion for weeks on end of small groups of men and women removed from their normal living circumstances creates an atmosphere conducive to romances, temporary or of longer duration, which are part of the colony's legend. Each colonist is given a bedroom and a shared bathroom in a residential building, plus a studio adapted to the colonist's specific art form. Music studios have grand pianos, art studios north light. Breakfast is served communally, and then lunch is taken in the studio – in fact the well-stocked lunchbox, delivered silently and punctually to every studio, has become one of the most enduring images of colony life. Equally distinctive is the practice of having colonists inscribe their names on plaques mounted on the studio walls, so that each newcomer enters into the history of his or her particular space. Dinners are served in the dining hall, and in earlier years there were regular Sunday dinners at Hillcrest with Mrs. MacDowell.

One of the few rules that had occasionally excited controversy during Mrs. MacDowell's tenure decreed that after dinner colonists were not permitted to return to their studios, ostensibly out of fear for their safety in the dark woods. Thus the colony's communal aspects came to the fore in the evenings, when the solitude of the day was replaced by discussion, readings, performances, and the like. However, this policy was changed several decades ago, and colonists now have full-time access to their working spaces.

In 1955 the colony began operating year-round, and 1960 saw the creation of the MacDowell Medal, awarded annually to a leading figure in the arts. In 1970 filmmakers began to be admitted to the colony; photographers followed in 1974 and architects in 1990. Today up to thirty-two artists are accommodated at one time.

The colony's illustrious history features major names in the arts, although the visual arts were somewhat less well represented than music and literature. When the colony published a list of former colonists in 1922 it included 89 writers, 33 composers, 19 performers, and 23 painters and sculptors. The visual artists included Lilla Cabot Perry, who had been a neighbor of Claude Monet's at Giverny and painted elegant portraits and impressionist landscapes (cat. no. 35); Glenn O. Coleman, a member of Robert Henri's circle of urban realists (cat. no. 12); and Jay Van Everen, a radical modernist whose paintings were inspired by cubism.[24] By 1955 the discrepancy was still evident: 436 of the former colonists had been writers, greatly outnumbering the 163 composers and 122 painters, sculptors, and printmakers.[25] A possible explanation for this unequal representation of visual artists is that they may be less inclined to leave the customized working environment of their own studios and transport all the necessary materials to stay in an art colony for a month or two. With fewer colonists in the visual arts, it is not surprising that fewer were of the stature of Milton Avery, who was a colonist for several summers, or of writers such as James Baldwin, Willa Cather, and Thornton Wilder, and composers Aaron Copland, Lukas Foss, and Leonard Bernstein. Though they were never colonists, such major artists as Willem de Kooning, Edward Hopper, and Jasper Johns did receive MacDowell Medals, and Ben Shahn served on admissions committees in the 1950s.

Nonetheless, a stay at the colony was of inestimable value to important American painters like O. Louis Guglielmi and Gregorio Prestopino (cat. nos. 22 and 38). Both wrote to Mrs. MacDowell expressing their gratitude for fellowships to the colony during financially difficult times. In Prestopino's words from 1934,

> I should be very willing to pay for my stay at Peterboro this year if I could, because I know how very much every bit of financial help means to the colony. But this year New York is even more cruel than usual to the artist who must make his living from day to day.

He also described the Adams studio, where he painted:

> Set, as it is, in the woods, and equipped with its large north-light window, it relieves the work of creation of many of its small struggles. Things like that make the Colony the perfect place for creative work.[26]

In subsequent years the colony has attracted artists of great accomplishment and stylistic diversity, from the abstract expressionist James Brooks to the realist Janet Fish (cat. nos. 9 and 17). It has also offered refuge and time for creative development to young painters who subsequently have risen to prominence in the art world, such as Louise Fishman and Glenn Ligon (cat. nos. 18 and 28). This is a function the MacDowell

Colony continues to fulfill as, today, in a time of lessening support for the arts nationwide, it moves into the twenty-first century with a committed group of supporters who are insuring that it will remain a unique and inspiring place for artists to work.

NOTES

1. The committee is quoted in Lawrence Gilman's *Edward MacDowell: A Study* (New York: Dodd, Mead and Company, 1908), p. 39. There is a vast amount of published and unpublished material about MacDowell and the colony. Lawrence Gilman was a music critic, an admirer of MacDowell's who became a friend; his monograph is one of the essential texts on the composer. Margery Morgan Lowens's well-researched and documented Ph.D. dissertation, "The New York Years of Edward MacDowell" (University of Michigan, 1971), is a valuable complement to Gilman.

2. Edward MacDowell, *New York Times*, 14 February 1904, p. 22.

3. Letter from the Trustees of Columbia College to Edward MacDowell, 8 March 1904, Marian MacDowell Papers, Library of Congress.

4. Gilman, *Edward MacDowell*, p. 54.

5. The official cause of his death was "'paresis' (dementia paralytica)"; Lowens, "The New York Years of Edward MacDowell," p. 558.

6. "The Passing of MacDowell," *Musical America*, February 1908, MacDowell clipping files, New York Public Library.

7. G.E.K., "A Fund for Edward MacDowell," *New York Times*, 15 November 1906, p. 7.

8. "MacDowell Fund Started," *New York Times*, 15 November 1906, sec. 9, p. 2.

9. "The MacDowell Fund," *New York Times*, 18 November 1906, sec. 10, p. 4.

10. Elsie Lathrop, "MacDowell Club Fosters All Arts," *Musical America*, 23 April 1910, p. 21. The Schola lasted through the 1950s.

11. *Prospectus*, MacDowell Club Papers, New-York Historical Society.

12. The artists who showed as the Eight were Arthur B. Davies, William Glackens, Robert Henri, Ernest Lawson, George Luks, Maurice Prendergast, Everett Shinn, and John Sloan. *The Exhibition of Independent Artists* was held in a rented building at 29–31 West 25th Street and featured works by 103 artists. Both shows were early manifestations of a rebellion against the restricted National Academy exhibitions that subsequently would include the MacDowell Club shows, the Armory Show, and the founding of the Society of Independent Artists in 1916. See William Inness Homer, "Henri and the Independent Movement," chap. 2 in *Robert Henri and His Circle* (New York: Hacker Art Books, 1988; 1st ed. 1969), pp. 126–56.

13. Sandra Leff, "Essay," *John White Alexander*, exh. cat., Graham Gallery (New York, 1980), p. 9.

14. "Living Pictures, and Artistic," *Saturday Post*, [?]16, 1906, MacDowell clipping files, New York Public Library.

15. John White Alexander, "Report of the President," *Annual Reports of the President and the Committees of the MacDowell Club of New York City*, April 1913, pp. 12–13.

16. Marian MacDowell Papers, Library of Congress. Most of the following information comes from these memoirs, which are also the principal source for Nancy McKee's biography of Mrs. MacDowell, *Valiant Woman* (San Antonio, Texas: The Naylor Company, 1962).

17. Marian MacDowell Papers, Library of Congress, reel 2.

18. Augustus Saint-Gaudens to Mrs. MacDowell, 10 November 1905, MacDowell Papers, Library of Congress.

19. "MacDowell Portrait Gains Fame for Author," Milwaukee, Wisconsin, newspaper, 20 February 1909, MacDowell clipping files, New York Public Library.

20. Mary Mears, "The Work and Home of Edward MacDowell, Musician," *The Craftsman* 16 (July 1909): 416–27.

21. "An American Pageant at an American Bayreuth," *New York Times*, 7 August 1910, p. 11.

22. For a good survey of the buildings at the colony see *The MacDowell Colony: A History of Its Architecture and Development* (Peterborough, N.H., 1981; reprinted 1988).

23. Hermann Hagedorn, "The Grand Old Lady of Peterborough," *New York Herald Tribune*, 22 November 1947.

24. "Who's Who at the MacDowell Colony," *The Edward MacDowell Association Bulletin*, no. 2, 1922, MacDowell Papers, Library of Congress, box 67.

25. *List of Artists Resident at the Colony*, 1910 to 1953 (New York: Edward MacDowell Association, Inc., 1953), MacDowell Papers, Library of Congress, box 67.

26. Gregorio Prestopino, two letters to Mrs. MacDowell, the first undated, the second 2 October 1934, MacDowell Papers, Library of Congress.

For their assistance on this essay I would like to thank Mary Carswell, Executive Director of the MacDowell Colony; Hollee Haswell, Curator of Columbiana, Columbia University; Dr. Monro Karetsky; Robert Saladini, Library of Congress; and Cheryl Wolf. T. W.

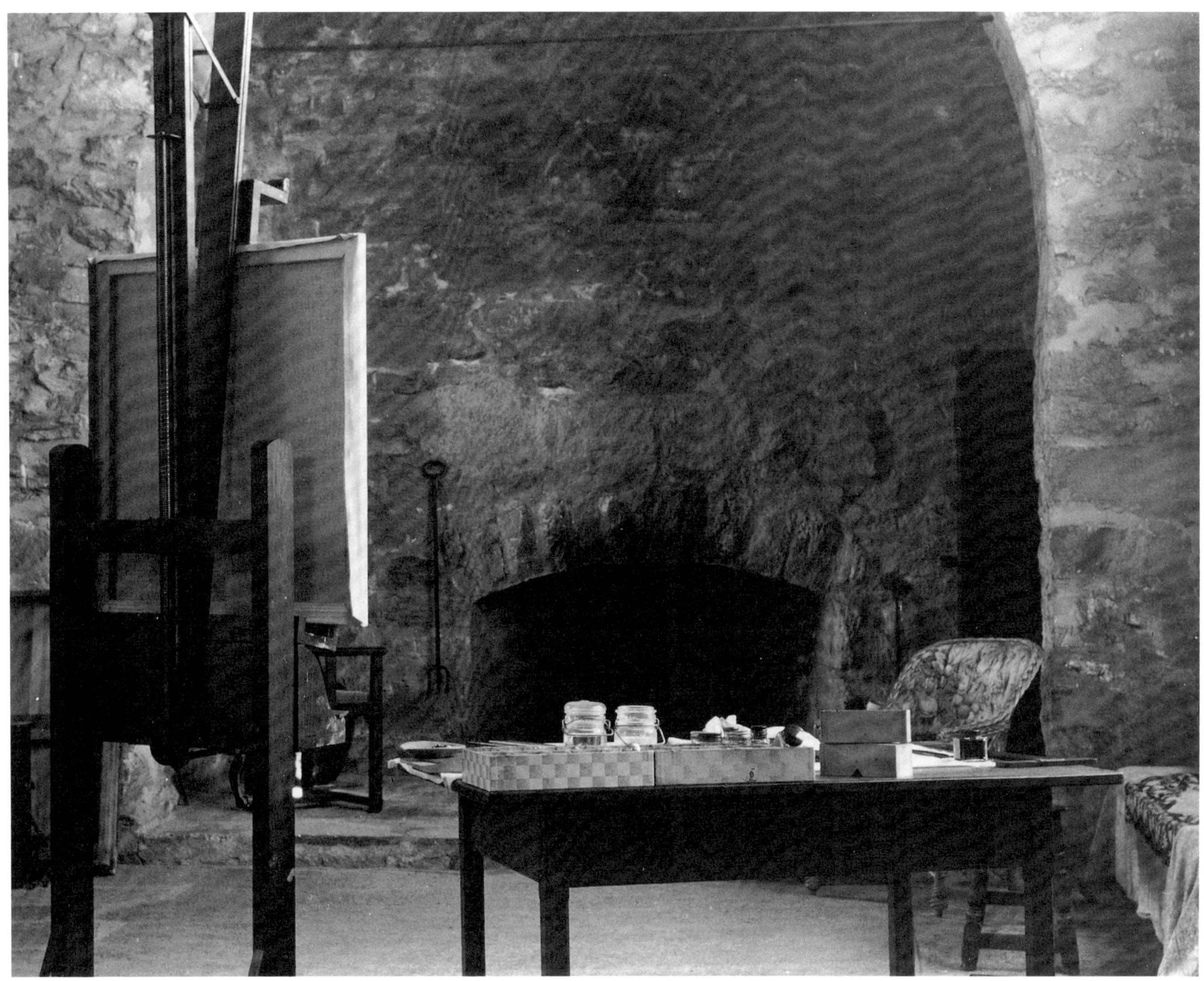

Interior of the Alexander Studio

A Parenthetical Place

Robert Storr

The currents of modern art are often hard to follow. It is the business of critics and historians to make them less so, and the self-appointed mission of others to give them clear direction, as if all aesthetic tributaries of any significance naturally coursed toward the grand flow of taste at a particular time. But modern art is not made for one reason but for many. Nor, in any period, does one destination beckon all its best talents. Where an artist works is frequently a matter of chance, and who she or he finds companionable in that context may well defy the theoretical rules of aesthetic association. Furthermore, as powerful as the pull of the art capitals may be, the sudden desire to get away from "the action" and the sometimes crushing sense of routine acceptance or rejection such places engender may be even more compelling.

For a great many years encompassing dramatic changes of style, poetic emphasis, or philosophical intent in American art, MacDowell has simultaneously offered itself as a place to be oneself, and *the* place to be in its own right, thus doubling as an art world unto itself and a temporary haven from the "art world" at large. The mark of its hospitality to individual creators is the great diversity of types it has welcomed over the years. Such diversity usefully draws attention to the many exceptions that exist to the generalizations in which art historians habitually traffic.

An account of American art based on those who came and went at MacDowell is, correspondingly, a patchwork rather than a comprehensive record, a vivid array instead of structured formal progressions of styles. Nonetheless, example by striking example, the broad design of American modernism remains discernible, and what's more, aspects often ignored in favor of those already well known claim a proportionately larger part of our attention. This shift in emphasis is a welcome corrective to our habits of eye and mind for two reasons: first, it foregrounds individuals as well as widely shared working assumptions that merit greater consideration on their own terms; second, it reframes our view of the "big picture" by widening its focus and filling in the blanks unnoticed because of our prior fixation on other, more conspicuous details.

Thus for instance, we may look back at the social realism of George Biddle and Gregorio Prestopino, and the social surrealism of O. Louis Guglielmi and be struck less by the formal conservatism of their pictorial language than by the unimpeachable straightforwardness with which they used it. Biddle's work (cat. no. 7) belongs to the documentary tradition of Depression-era art, but the harshness of what he sees is softened by the "humanist" tenderness of his painterly touch, while the comparative crispness of Prestopino's images (cat. no. 38) and the careful grouping and isolation of the figures in them hymns small town individualism and egalitarianism with the spareness of a Woody Guthrie tune. In the long historical interval since these works were made, our faith that "this land is our land" has been badly shaken; but after all, Guthrie first sang his song to convince his dispossessed public that they still had a stake in their future, knowing full well how tenuous their hold upon it was becoming. Which is to say that his talking-blues were always more a matter of hopeful talk than of straight talk. Prestopino's sentiments, like those of Biddle, seem old-fashioned in the same way; but they are not to be scorned, and they do remind us that at one time the myth of community self-determination in this country was not primarily the possession of the far-right.

Guglielmi's (cat. no. 22) is the stranger and more compelling artistic vision, however; his synthesis of neoromantic ambiance, fragmentary narrative, and classical composition applied to the urban desolation of thirties America was an idiosyncratic endeavor. As picture-poetry, it is, nonetheless, convincing, perhaps more convincing now than when the streets and interiors of New York reflected this dilapidation, for in the final analysis it is the uncanny or magical quality of Guglielmi's scenarios that linger in the mind, rather than the actuality upon which they were partially based.

In marked aesthetic contrast to realism, if not in direct ideological opposition to it, nonobjective painting flourished in the 1930s and 1940s largely under the aegis of the American Abstract Artists, the oldest group of its kind, here represented by a quartet of artists. The first, Esphyr Slobodkina (cat. no. 43), was and still is a living link to the Russian avant-garde of the 1920s; the second, Charmion von Wiegand (cat. no. 48), represented a direct connection to Mondrian, whom she befriended during his brief stay in New York from 1940 to 1944. Like those of Irene Rice Pereira, the third in this group, von Wiegand's paintings are distinguished by lucid, at times atmospheric geometries quite distinct from the more solidly structured shapes and spaces of Slobodkina and Alice Trumbull Mason, the group's fourth member. Among them, however, they demonstrate the variety of approaches that were taken in the name of pure abstraction, making that austere program seem, if not less pure in fact than in theory, then less predictable than its stated tenets implied. Thus, for example, Alice Trumbull Mason (cat. no. 30) took the floating bars and blocks of Mondrian's austere "plus-minus" works and infused them with rich mixed reds, browns, oranges, and blues of a kind that were anathema to the Dutch master. For her part, Pereira (cat. no. 34) enlarged similar compositional elements but modulated them by applying the pigment in scraped, inconsistently dense layers, violating yet another article of the neo-plasticist doctrine, but finding a more open painterly horizon as a result. One final observation on this score: in an art world now acutely conscious of gender and largely inclined to think of the art world of the past as having been an exclusively male precinct, it is worth emphasizing that all four of these artists were women, and that, as was the case in Russia, and to a lesser degree in Poland and Germany, nonobjective art seemed to attract a high proportion of women, as well as men who dealt with them as equals.

Abstract expressionism was, famously, a boys' club. Legendary aggressions against images and materials are its legacy. In reality, though, the violent exertions of Pollock and de Kooning constituted only one dimension of their multidimensional work, and their work was only a part of a many-faceted artistic tendency. James Brooks (cat. no. 9), Pollock's close friend, lent to the common language of gestural painting in the 1950s a graphic lyricism and lushness of color all his own. Where Pollock's tracery line alternately raced or skipped across his canvases, Brooks's washes swelled into elegant forms, while his fluttering hand agitated their surface, making fine tonal variations. Also a colorist, Giorgio Cavallon (cat. no. 11) infused the shifting planar syntax of hard-edged nonobjective painting with a brilliant atmospheric glow whose principal effect was to eat away at those hard edges, just as the sun at certain angles adds shimmer to but erodes the contours of the shapes it illuminates. Thus Cavallon let a diffuse Mediterranean light in on the sharply defined red, white, blue, yellow, and black universe of the northern Mondrian and his New World followers. The expressionism of Paul Burlin's improvisational painting (cat. no. 10) is more pronounced, by comparison, though it shares with Cavallon's a particular chromatic saturation more European than American in tone. But then, abstract expressionism was the first great thriving hybrid in art to result from the grafting of American branches onto European roots; it was the meeting place of old settlers and new immigrants in a country where almost everything cultivated in native soil came from somewhere else.

In the thick, churning paintings of the contemporary painter Louise Fishman (cat. no. 18), abstract expressionism is brought up to date and adapted to new requirements. Although it plainly acknowledges its heritage, hers is not a nostalgic exercise. Instead, the artist has used precedent as point of departure for a kind of picture-making more condensed than what came before, as if the expansiveness previously inbred in American abstract art was being called into question, and a weightier, less optimistic vision had taken its place. However, Fishman's work continues to affirm the basic abstract expressionist idea that spirit reveals itself in matter, and though that spirit may carry an added burden of history its conviction has not suffered as a consequence. In the work of Candida Alvarez (cat. no. 1), the specters and mists one associates with the color-field side of abstract expressionism – with Baziotes and Rothko in particular, and with Loren McIver a little further in the background – give birth to new images at once intimate in quality and just out of direct interpretive reach. Which is to say that one feels them in all their nuance but cannot fully account for them. Alvarez further complicates things by abutting two quite differently articulated panels, inserting into the lower one a figurative detail. And so the juxtapositional strategies of painting in the 1980s meet those of symbolic abstraction in a distinctive mix that keeps one's gaze moving back and forth between subtle contrasts while it keeps one guessing what it is that seems to simultaneously dissolve and coalesce like thoughts or memories at the edge of sleep.

Just as the tectonic color plates of Fishman's painting seem drawn inward by pressures upon them, the bound filaments in Carol Hepper's sculpture (cat. no. 24) twist and turn back on themselves, creating a physical knot with distinct emotional overtones. This work also recalls the organic shapes typical of so much American art in the 1950s, but the straightforward way in which they are brought together and the simplicity with which they are manipulated is more characteristic of the process art of the late 1960s and early 1970s. There is in fact no illusion and no overt symbolism, just the heightened tension of clustered elements bent into a single continuous coil. Somewhere between a spring and a muscle, Hepper's work contains its strength but might, it appears, release it at any moment. The symmetrically arranged halves of John Newman's sculpture (cat. no. 33) possess the same potential, joined as they are by twined ropes, but Newman's paradigms are molecular rather than "biomorphic" in the usual sense of that surrealist-inspired term. Just as certain aspects of minimalism tapped into systems theory, and other tendencies that emerged in the 1960s and 1970s transposed images and ideas from the natural sciences, Newman has given scale to shapes and their dynamics of a sort we would expect to see only with the aid of advanced laboratory equipment. Not that Newman is illustrating the "micro" in "macro" proportions. Nor do his invented "whatsits" literally derive from physics or biology; rather they bear a relation to contemporary science similar to the one that Theodore Roszak's streamlined sculpture of the 1930s bore to modern engineering. Advances in research or technology produce new forms or give us access to forms previously beyond our ken; the contribution that art makes is to see in these practical discoveries things that have never existed and serve no other purpose than those of the imagination. Newman knows this, and lets his imagination go, tracking the increasingly baroque permutations of his invented structures as if those changes described natural eclosion of living things.

Meanwhile, careful observation of the given world has yielded a new generation of realists in recent years. More dispassionate on the whole than the social realists of the past, they tend to stick close to home, and close to the facts as they find them. Among the most prosaic of such artists is Janet Fish (cat. no. 17), who takes things pretty much as they come and, by giving them her full attention, restores to the everyday objects our glance normally passes over the substance they truly have. Thus goods plastic-wrapped for rapid purchase and consumption achieve a kind of monumentality and permanence that makes us see the beauty in them. That beauty is "nothing special," but the fact that we have been made to stop and notice it is special. Marjorie Portnow (cat. no. 37) approaches the landscape with the same patient equanimity as Fish approaches the produce department at the grocery store, and so too does Altoon Sultan (cat. no. 45). The so-called romantic fallacy consists of projecting human moods and notions onto nature; Portnow and Sultan are content to let nature and the human imprint upon it look in their pictures pretty much as they look in reality. Correspondingly, the light in their skies is devoid of theatrical enhancements since all it needs to do is show us the scene as one would see it on a normal day. The artifice in their work is present in the apparent lack of any; this much painterly discretion takes skill and discipline. It is the aesthetic equivalent of laconic Yankee understatement in practical matters, which is why it rings so true when directed toward the description of Yankee ground. Helen Miranda Wilson (cat. no. 51) belongs in this company as well, but strays from it to the extent that she grants herself poetic license to dissolve one minutely scrutinized image into another or to find archetypes in commonplace scenes or objects. Gregory Gillespie (cat. no. 21) goes further still in this direction. Accurately limned in each detail, his paintings as an accumulation of superabundant details assume a claustrophobic aspect that soon spills over into hallucinatory excess and disjunction, suggesting the chance encounter of Edgar Allan Poe and William Burroughs in a setting imagined by Hieronymus Bosch.

The fantastic is also an element in Benny Andrews's work (cat. no. 2). On the one hand harkening back to social realism in its narrative dimensions, on the other Andrews indulges in a slyly revealing whimsy that places his portraits somewhere between affectionate caricature and pure formal play of pattern and color. Faith Ringgold (cat. no. 42) is also a storyteller with a keen sense of how eloquently decoration speaks of its origins and uses. Using the quilting tradition so long relegated to the secondary status of craft, she combines and contrasts folk designs, icons from the modernist tradition, and wholly contemporary motifs to create compositions that boldly affirm the multiplicity of cultures in America in lieu of arguing the point. That those cultures at times clash visually in her work as they do in reality is simply a fact of life. Ringgold thus replaces the proverbial melting pot with a cloth of many colors, and one takes pleasure in the vibrancy of the results not least because one can take satisfaction in the truthfulness of that metaphorical substitution.

Glenn Ligon (cat. no. 28), one of the youngest artists in the show, names the reality in the background of the work of Ringgold and Andrews, and that reality is race. However, racial consciousness in this country is not a simple matter of fact but rather a complex one of perceptions, of the recognition of others as "different" and of self-recognition, and what one makes of all that. "I feel most colored when I am thrown against a sharp white background," reads the text Ligon has borrowed from Zora Neale Hurston for his word-picture. Forcing soft, waxy paint through a stencil, Ligon subjects this text to a painterly technique that causes it to break down so that the clear distinction between black and white to which the line refers begins to blur. This process does not suggest the felicitous integration of the two extremes so much as anxiety-driven and anxiety-producing confusion born of the rote repetition of this idea. The more one insists on the absolute opposition of supposedly dichotomous terms the harder that separation is to maintain and to endure. Adding landscapist Richard Mayhew (cat. no. 31) and watercolorist Richard Yarde (cat. no. 52) to the list of artists included in this exhibition, one can see that in an art world only intermittently open to African Americans, MacDowell has consistently welcomed talent without prejudice.

It is the work – not background, beliefs, or aesthetic allegiance – that gains an artist entry to MacDowell's quiet woods and solitary studios. That is as it should be. Vehement contention among ideas and the competition of styles happens in the wider world. (And that, too, is as it should be.) Inside this small community with its rotating population, however, the art that will eventually have to stand on its own is prepared and created in an atmosphere of respect and trust. The exchanges that occur in that environment among men and women of utterly different experience and aims are subtle but significant since they are the product of those rare times when people gather according to their differences rather than their similarities. Looked at that way, the pictures in this exhibition form a kind of prism through which one can perceive otherwise hard-to-see points of contact between separate tendencies in American art, knowing that for a brief period artists who normally would not have met one another spent a month or more in the country together. If the dates when those artists represented in this show were actually present at MacDowell do not exactly correlate – and regrettably there are too many to name them all or describe every work in detail – then think that at any given time a comparably heterogeneous and accomplished group would have been in residency. Whatever the precise circumstances or interval of their time at MacDowell, artists who have been there have been changed by it. An exception to their normal routines and a respite from the pressures to which they are usually accustomed, MacDowell represents a major parenthesis in the creative lives of all who have had the good fortune to go, qualifying their work in significant ways while they are there, and continuing to affect it long afterwards. Not infrequently they return for another stay, and another, in which case these breaks can be read as part of the basic rhythm of their artistic growth. Likewise, as the examples in this exhibition attest, the painting and sculpture made by MacDowell artists opens an important parenthesis in the history of American art. It remains open.

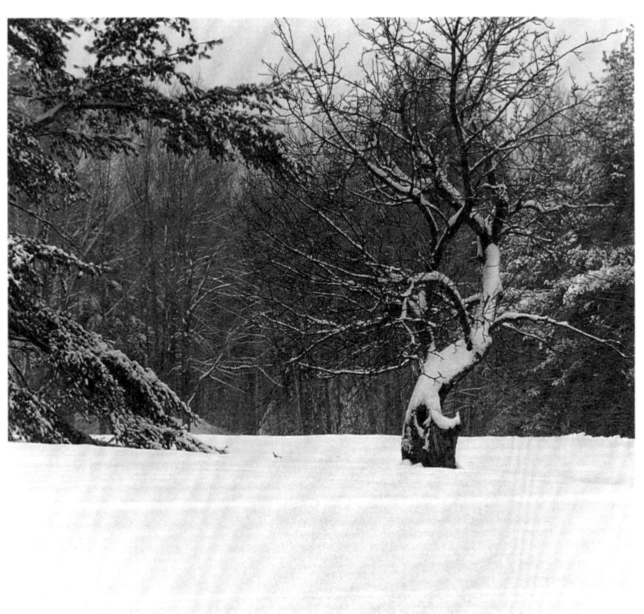

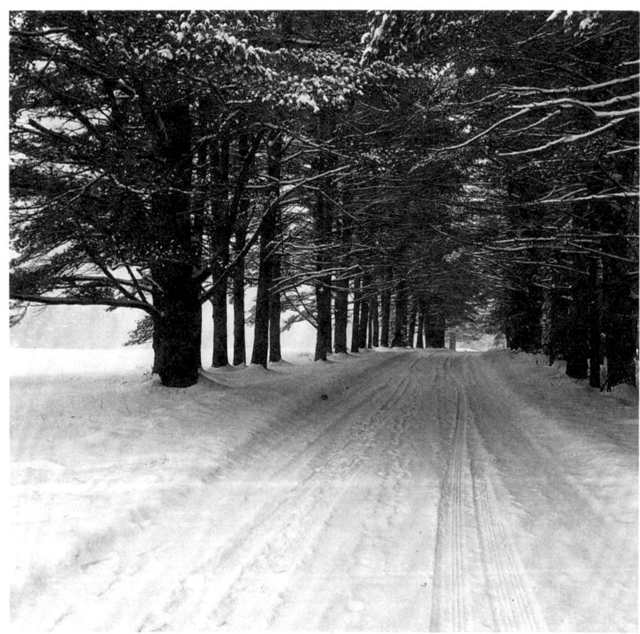

Artists' Statements

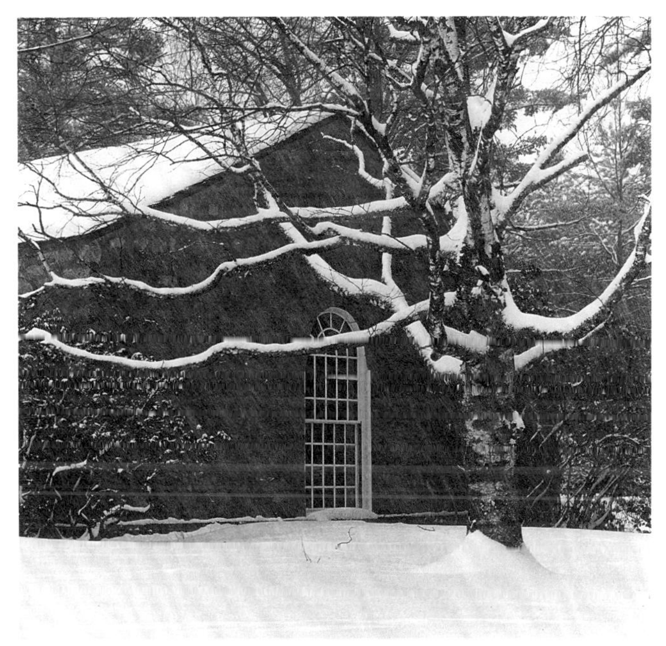

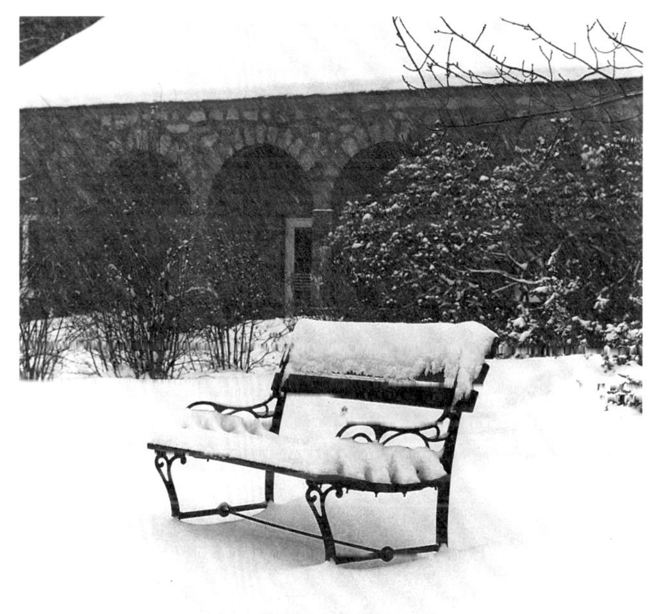

NATURE IS MY SPRINGBOARD. From her I get my initial impetus. I have tried to relate the visible drama of mountains, trees, and bleached fields with the fantasy of winds blowing and changing colors and forms. The MacDowell Colony provided the perfect habitat for all this to happen naturally.

—MILTON AVERY
about 1955

Nature is my springboard.
From her I get my initial impetus.

. . . for the first time I felt I was in a community of people who not only tolerated me but who understood and supported my need to work long hours.

WHAT I VALUED MOST about being at MacDowell was the freedom from all responsibility and problems and concerns that normally to some degree sap my creative energy. I enjoyed the feeling of privacy – of unlimited, uninterrupted time which enabled me to work with more concentrated effort for longer periods of time than I had ever found possible in my actual situation, as a husband, a father, and a householder.

For my kind of work, which is very detailed and takes a lot of patient effort, the result was liberating. I felt I could really sink into the pieces – I felt less rushed than I've ever felt in my life. Also, for the first time I felt I was in a community of people who not only tolerated me but who understood and supported my need to work long hours.

—GREGORY GILLESPIE
1978

I HAVE HAD THREE RESIDENCIES at MacDowell, in the summers of 1987, 1989, and 1990. These stays were important to my ability to adapt to living in New York City after moving here from a very rural part of South Dakota. Going to New Hampshire was a welcome respite from the city, allowing me to reconnect with nature. It is no wonder, then, that the arrival of the hot days in the city now creates the urge to take the drive to Peterborough for the summer.

The residencies at MacDowell gave me the invaluable opportunity to meet and spend time with a group of artists from all disciplines for an extended period. My experience in New York until then had been primarily with visual artists. Sitting down to breakfast and dinner every day with the same people and picking up on or continuing discussions and stories, I formed some of my most intimate and lasting friendships. Each stay was made unique by the mix of artists. It was stimulating to be with peers while we made work that was later to be exhibited or published. To be able to see and hear their work in progress, to be in such close communication with them, made the works almost speak with the sound of their creators' voices when I later saw or read them, far removed from the context of the colony. Those pieces vibrated with the resonance of that time and place.

The remarkable staff made each stay a pleasure, with their thoughtfulness and their good-natured solutions to various problems. Going out of their way to help us set up the most productive and comfortable, if not familiar, working environment, they would find tables for the studio and search out more comfortable chairs or arrange the removal of old ones. The first days after arrivals often looked like a game of musical chairs.

One of the most unusual aspects was getting used to having lunch delivered to the doorstep of the studio everyday just before noon – in a picnic basket! I soon found myself anticipating the sound of the pick-up truck driving up the dirt road, and trying to guess what that day's basket would hold.

Because of this invigorating and nurturing environment, I was always very productive at the colony, usually outpacing what I was able to produce in my New York studio during the same period. The atmosphere was geared toward the studio. With uninterrupted privacy, days felt longer and one month seemed like three because of the focused quality of time. I also found myself taking big risks with my work, having the time and focus to push through and resolve some of the problems that may have otherwise followed the work for quite some time.

After many productive days in the studio and the feeling that there would be many more, a group of us would bicycle out to Willard Pond for a swim in the late afternoon before returning for dinner. The feeling of rejuvenation and accomplishment would stay with me long after I returned to New York.

—CAROL HEPPER
1996

The picnic basket lunch, a MacDowell Colony tradition.

I also found myself taking big risks with my work, having the time and focus to push through and resolve some of the problems that may have otherwise followed the work for quite some time.

I AM INDEBTED to this fine Eden known as MacDowell. Each of my three stays at the colony has played a strong part in how I have come to define myself as an artist, helped me through the rough spots, and given me a solid base which is vital to anyone who takes on such a potentially precarious career.

My first stay was over a period of eight warm weeks in the summer of 1988. There were changes from the start. For one, the sheer breadth and physical beauty of the colony rapidly moved into my canvases. Prior to this I had never understood the potential narrative power of the landscape I was actively living in. Secondly, owing to the uninterrupted time for work, I began to make vital priorities in my life outside the colony, eager to preserve that sense of peace of mind I had rediscovered and ready to pursue a second career in teaching, which I had previously felt apprehensive about. There is no equal to the richness I found in my friendships with and exposure to the other colonists. MacDowell provides the time to know ourselves and each other in ways so rarely encountered in our everyday lives.

During my second residency in the fall of 1989, I held on to a distracted mood. The honeymoon was over and my sense of self-doubt more weighty. But in the end the finished paintings were surprisingly strong, and again the colony played a large role in that. The lush New England fall was overwhelming, the new friendships of invaluable depth, and that quality of trust which seems to pervade the studio helped me grasp that I was indeed doing something of value. By my last visit in the winter of 1993, I was now one of many teachers working there on borrowed time. We all worked hard as the snow fell continuously, and I experienced my first "Canadian picnic" outside one January day.

Thinking of You (cat. no. 23) still holds me on many levels. For one, it stems from that first magical stay in 1988 when I discovered the richness of landscape. The chair was that of another colonist who treasured this open area near her more wooded studio. I can still mentally sit in that chair and re-experience all the sensations of the colony at its meditative and reflective best. But the meaning goes farther back for me personally in a longing for fading spaces and some good souls who are no longer around.

MacDowell remains irresistible in its nurturing atmosphere and in that sense of well-being that comes to you, giving you the time to stretch and grow and scratch out and throw out and then, finally, preserve that piece which was previously so difficult to express. This is an invaluable gift.

—SUSAN HAMBLETON
1996

Prior to this I had never understood the potential narrative power of the landscape I was actively living in.

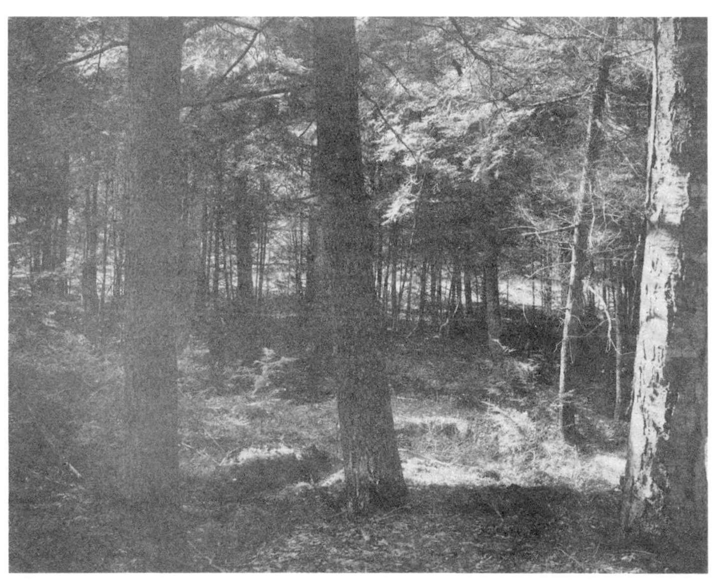

What a great spirit lingers in this place!

THE MACDOWELL COLONY

What a great spirit lingers in this place!
Broad as the sky and gentle as a flower,
Here his white flame burned through its too short hour
Beneath tall pines that arch and interlace.
Perhaps this very branch has touched his face
That brushes now my own. These trees that tower
Above me, echoed once his music's power,
And through all time his memory shall retrace.

He found in this log cabin flecked with shade
Refuge from the world's clamor. Here were born
His noblest harmonies . . . and his last prayer
Was that through coming years others might share
This healing, where he had made
Fresh pathways leading to a brighter morn.

—LILLA CABOT PERRY

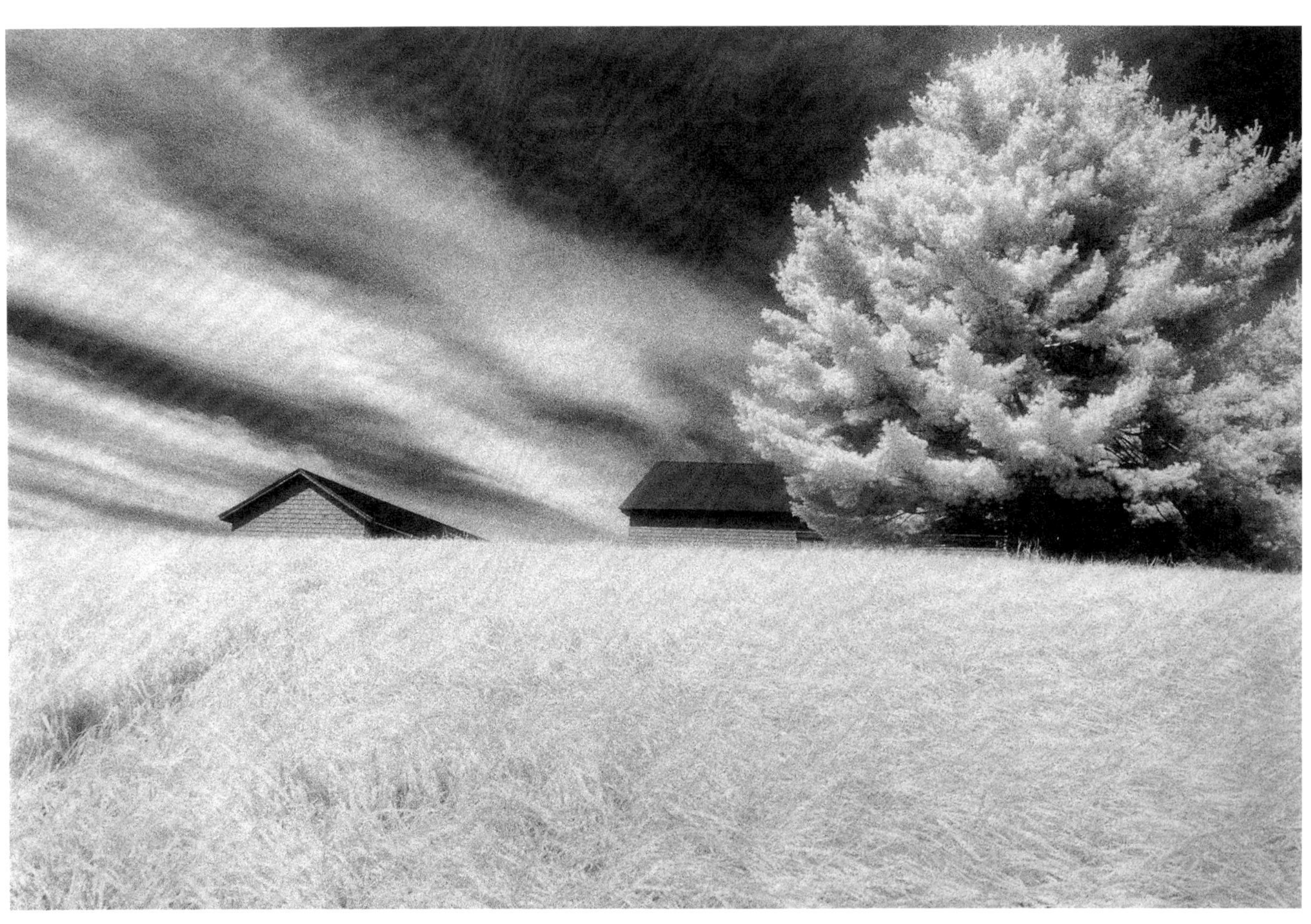

Catalogue of the Exhibition

All dimensions are in inches; height is followed by width, and where appropriate, by depth.

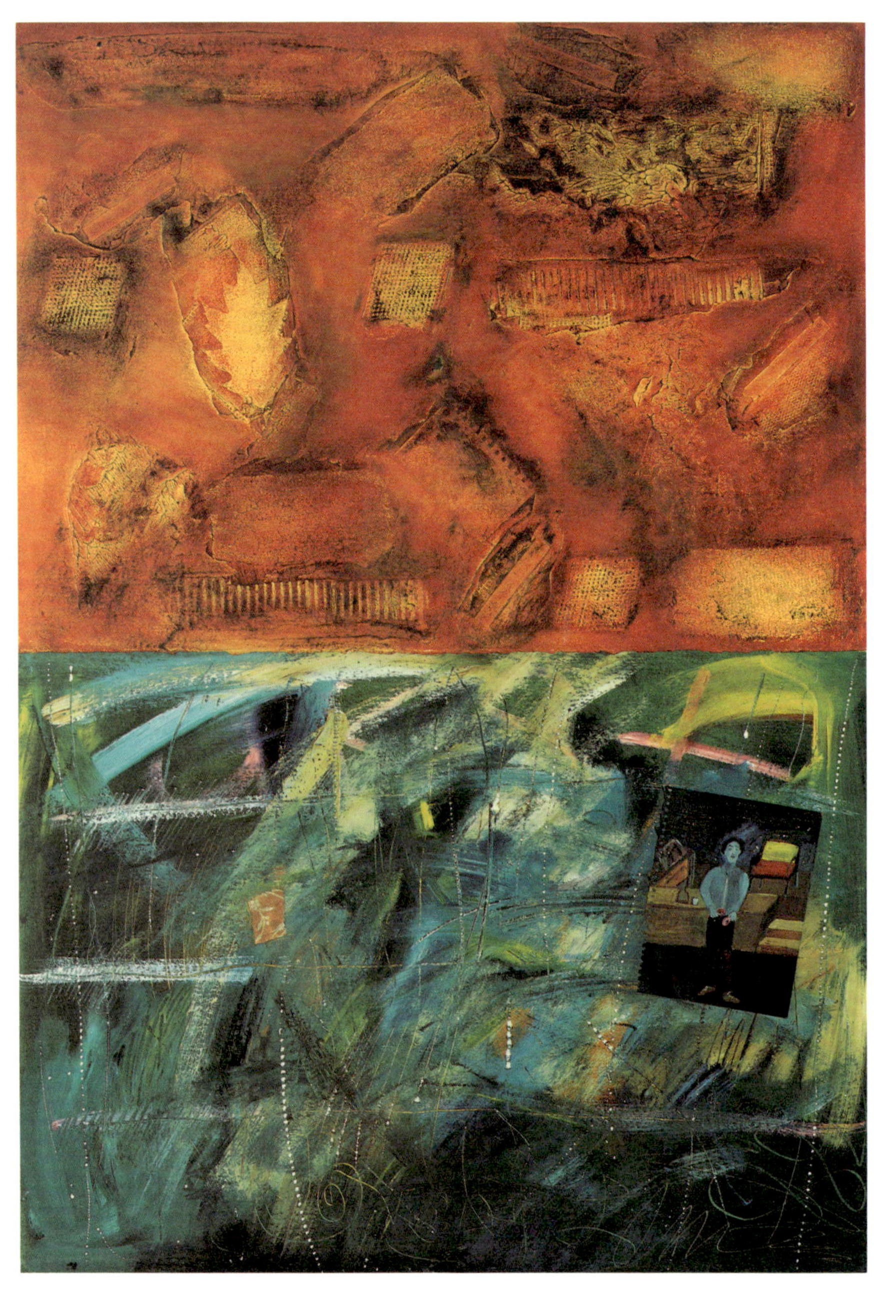

I

CANDIDA ALVAREZ (b. 1955)
Max Playing the Maracas, 1986

Acrylic on paper, 44 × 30¾
Collection of the Artist; Courtesy June Kelly Gallery, New York

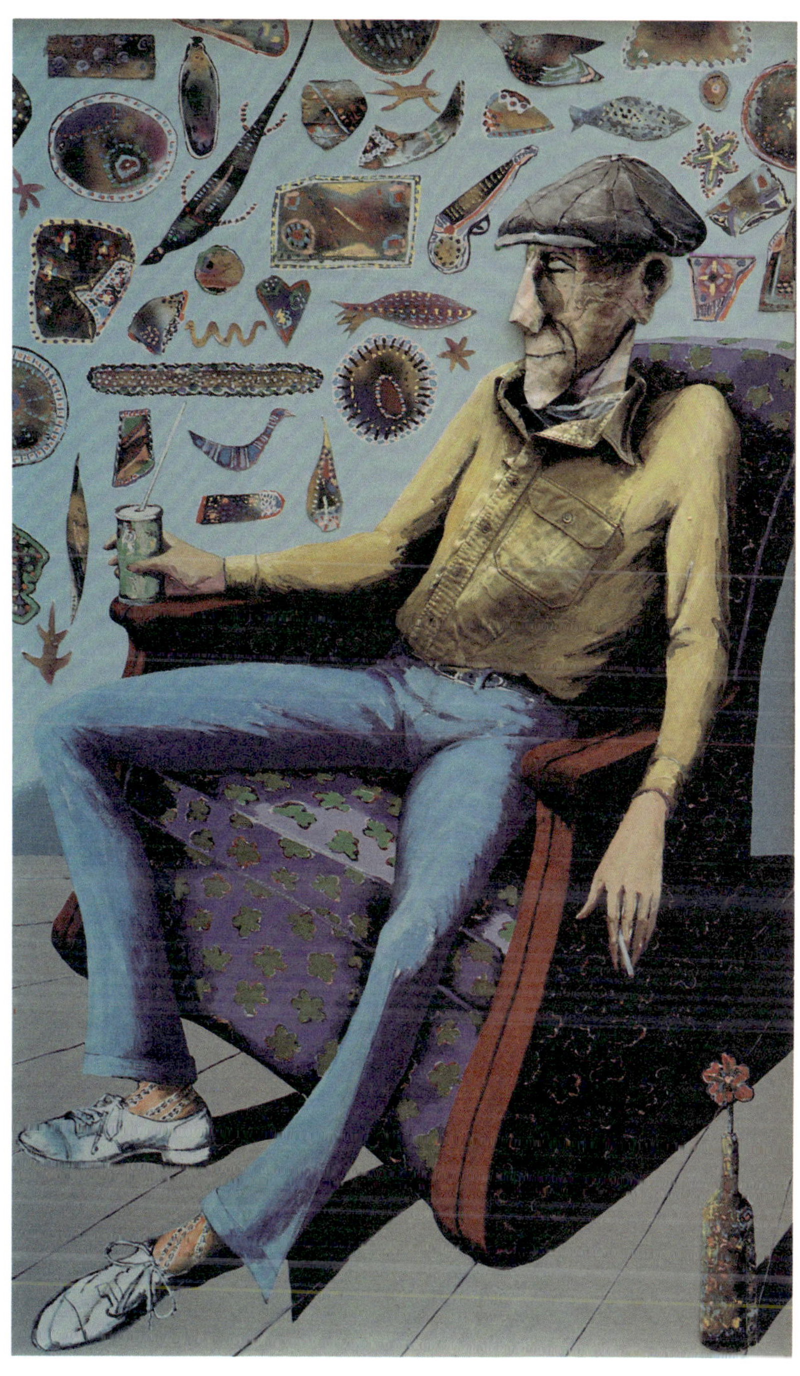

2

BENNY ANDREWS (b. 1930)
Portrait of George Andrews, 1986
Oil and collage on canvas, 85 × 51
Collection of the Artist

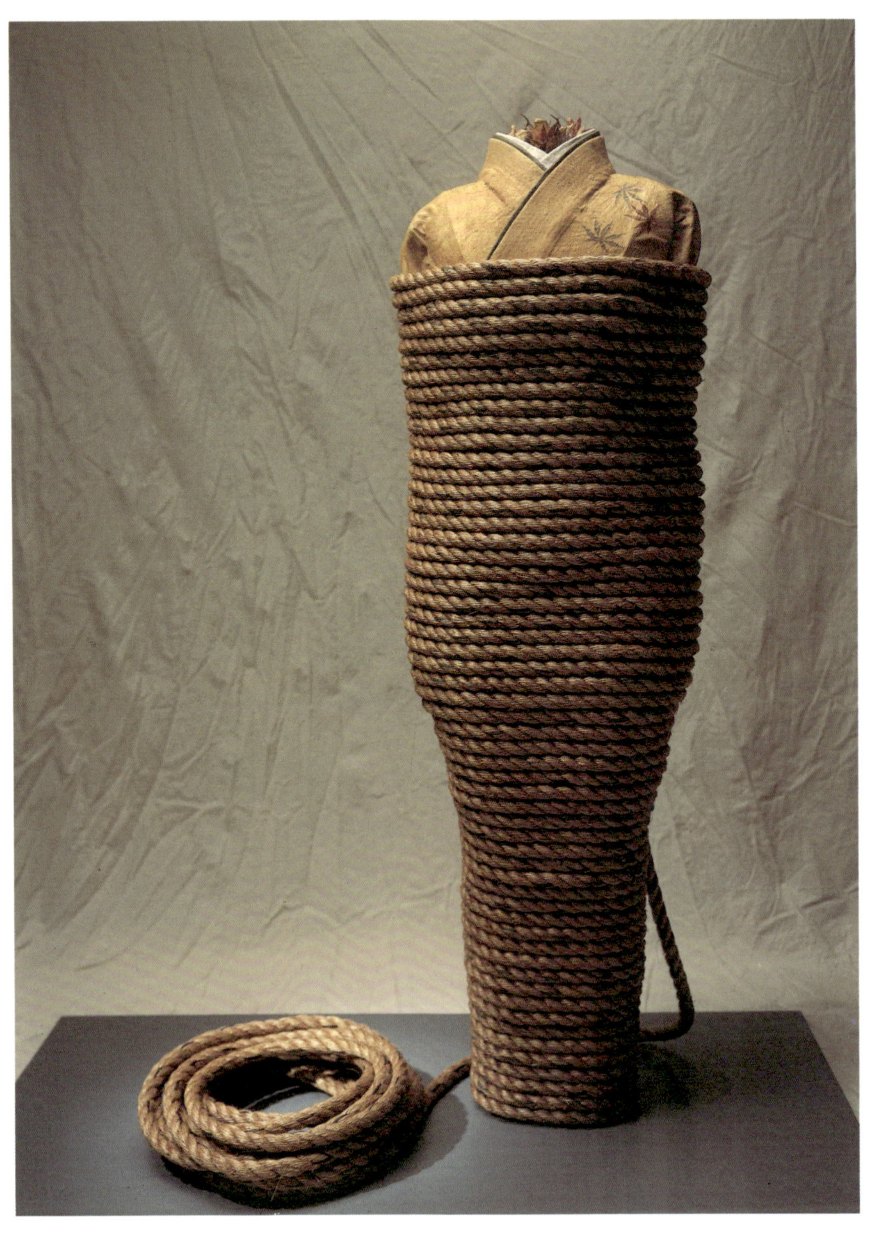

3
KRISTINE YUKI AONO (b. 1960)
Rope Kimono II, 1996
Rope, "Design Cast" plaster fabric, wood, wire mesh, styrofoam, pigment, Japanese and North American maple leaves, 54 × 48 × 24
Collection of the Artist

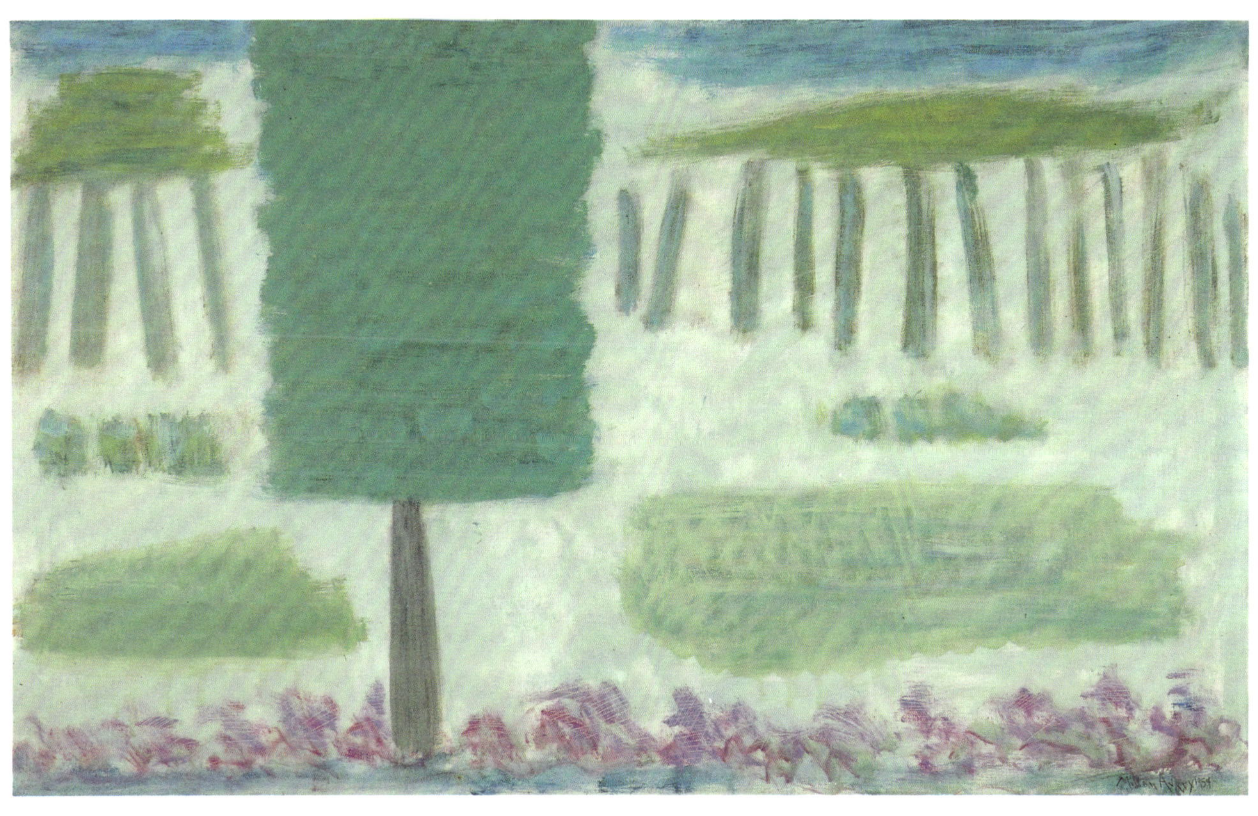

4
MILTON AVERY (1885–1965)
Spring in New Hampshire, 1954
Oil on canvas, 34 × 58
Milton Avery Trust; Courtesy Wright Gallery, New York

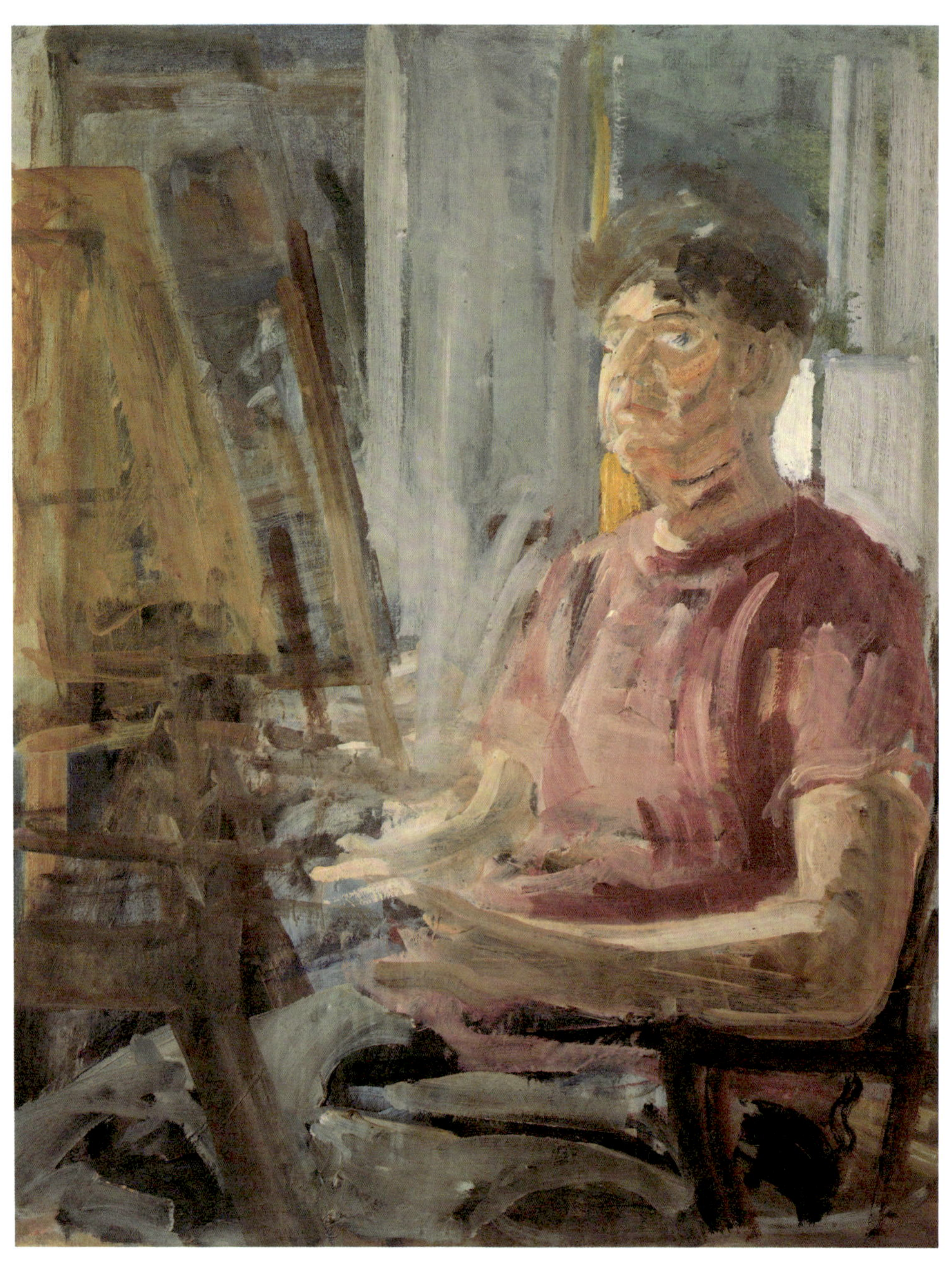

5
LELAND BELL (1922–1991)
Self-Portrait at Easel, 1954
Oil on board, 24 × 19
Courtesy Salander-O'Reilly Galleries, New York

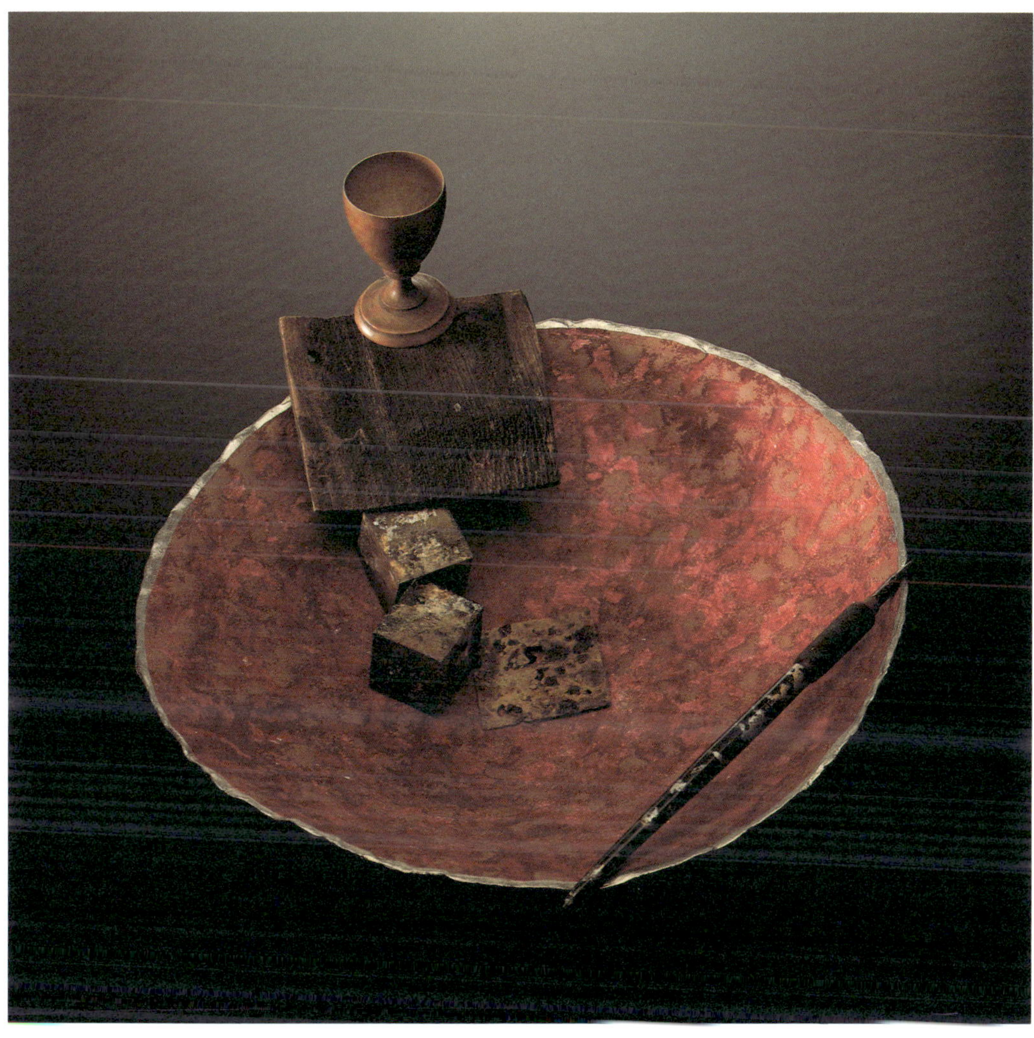

6

CHRISTINA BERTONI (b. 1945)

Wooden Cup, 1992

Earthenware, acrylic paint, and found objects, 7 × 11 × 11

Collection of the Artist

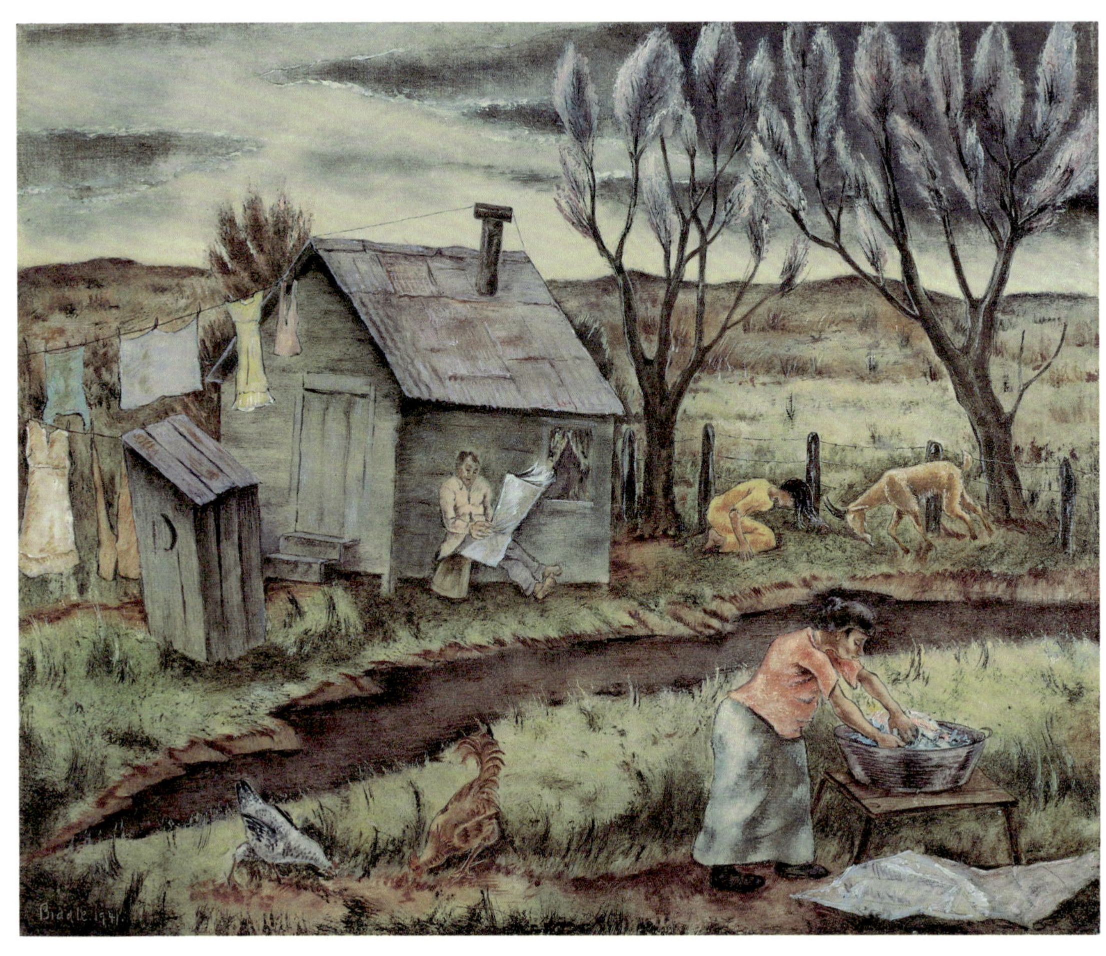

7
GEORGE BIDDLE (1885–1973)
Tortilla Flat in Spring, 1941
Oil on canvas, 25 × 30
Collection of Patricia and Donald Oresman

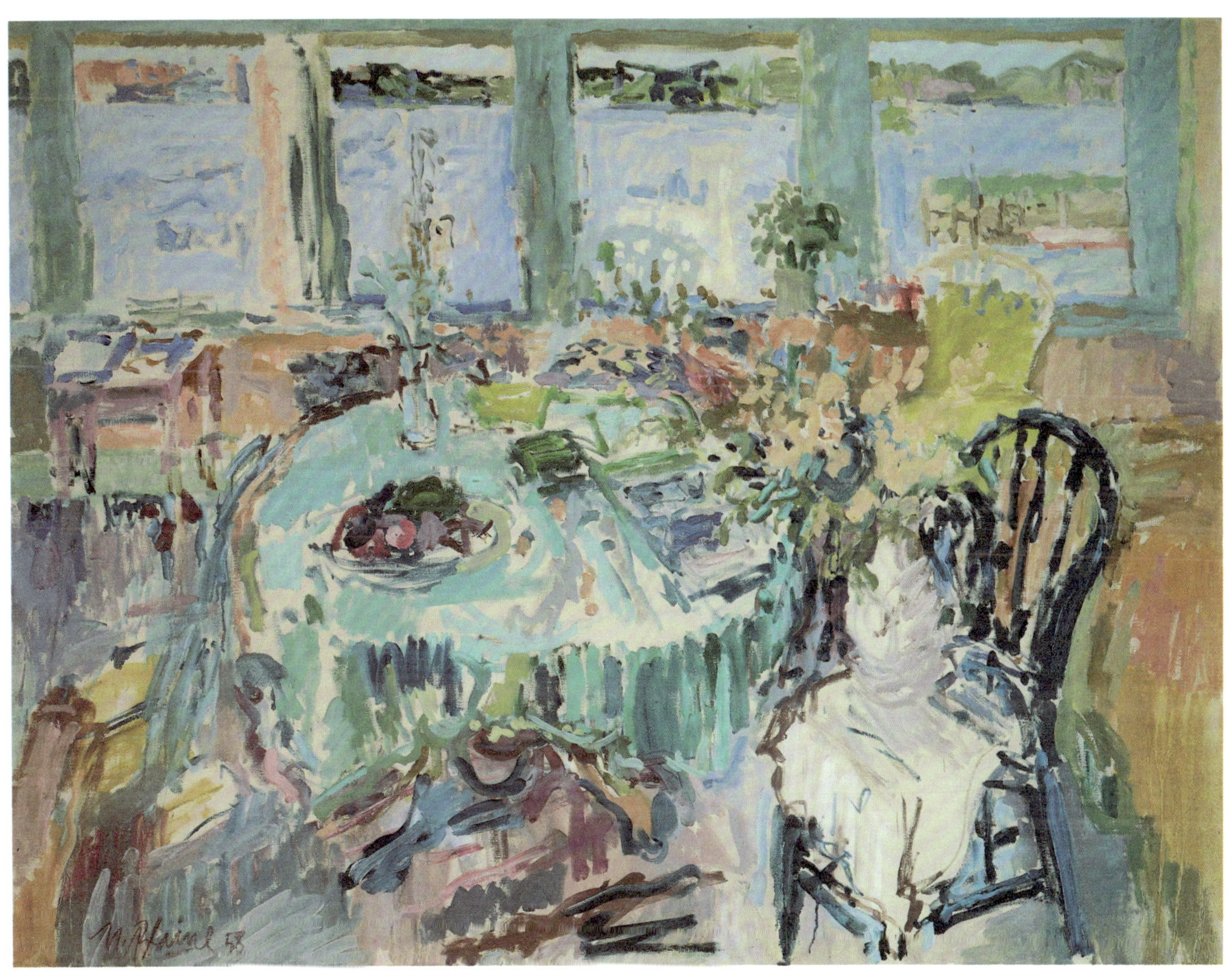

8

NELL BLAINE (b. 1922)
Harbor and Green Cloth II, 1958

Oil on canvas, 50 × 65
Whitney Museum of American Art, New York;
Purchase, with funds from the Neysa McMein Purchase Award

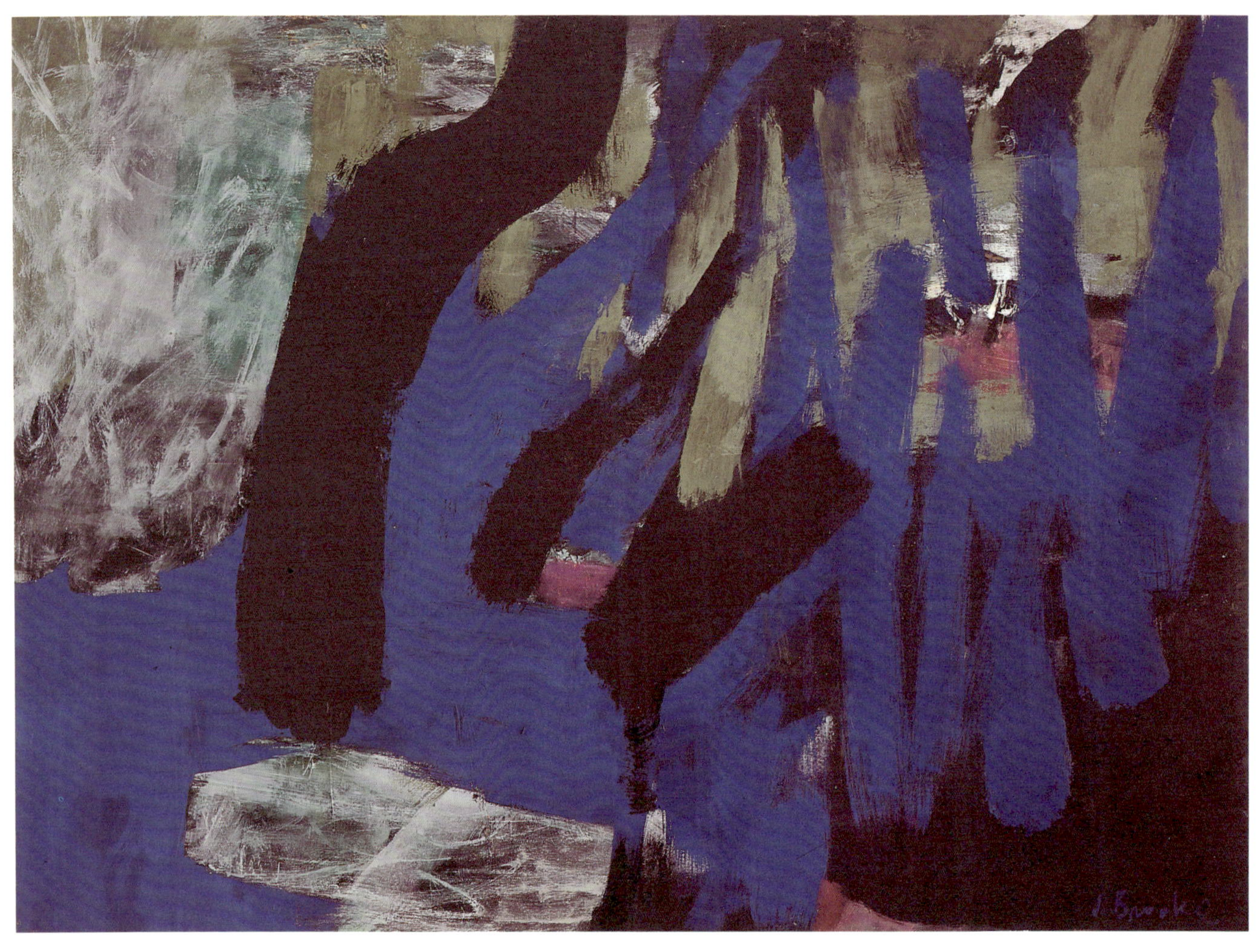

9
JAMES BROOKS (1906–1992)
Rodado, 1961
Oil on canvas, 57 × 78
Rose Art Museum, Brandeis University, Waltham, Massachusetts;
Gevirtz-Mnuchin Purchase

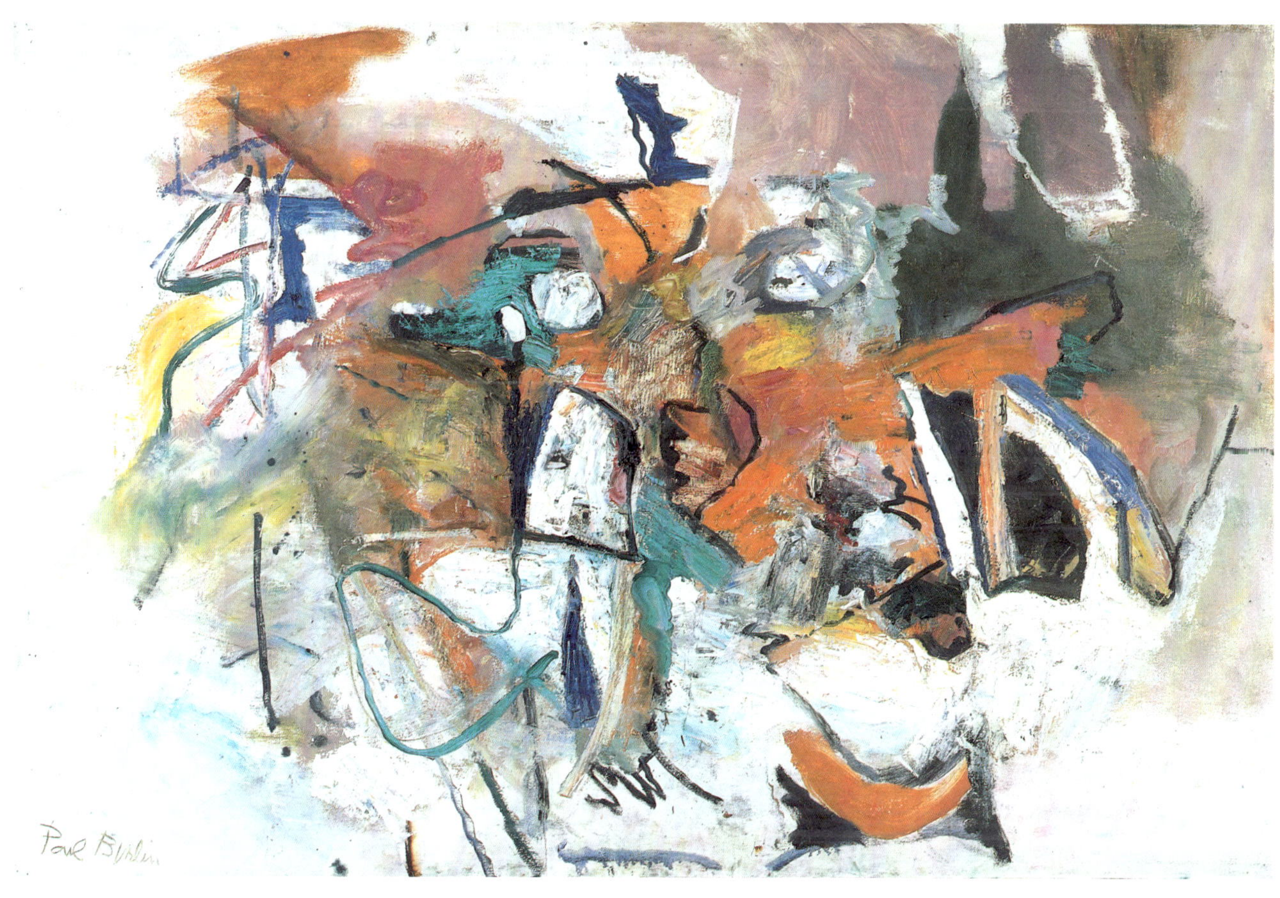

10

PAUL BURLIN (1886–1969)

Red, Red, Not the Same, 1959

Oil on canvas, 48¼ × 72

Whitney Museum of American Art, New York; Gift of Sam Jaffe, Milton Lowenthal, Harry Pinkerson, Bernard Reis, and Dr. Samuel Ernest Sussman

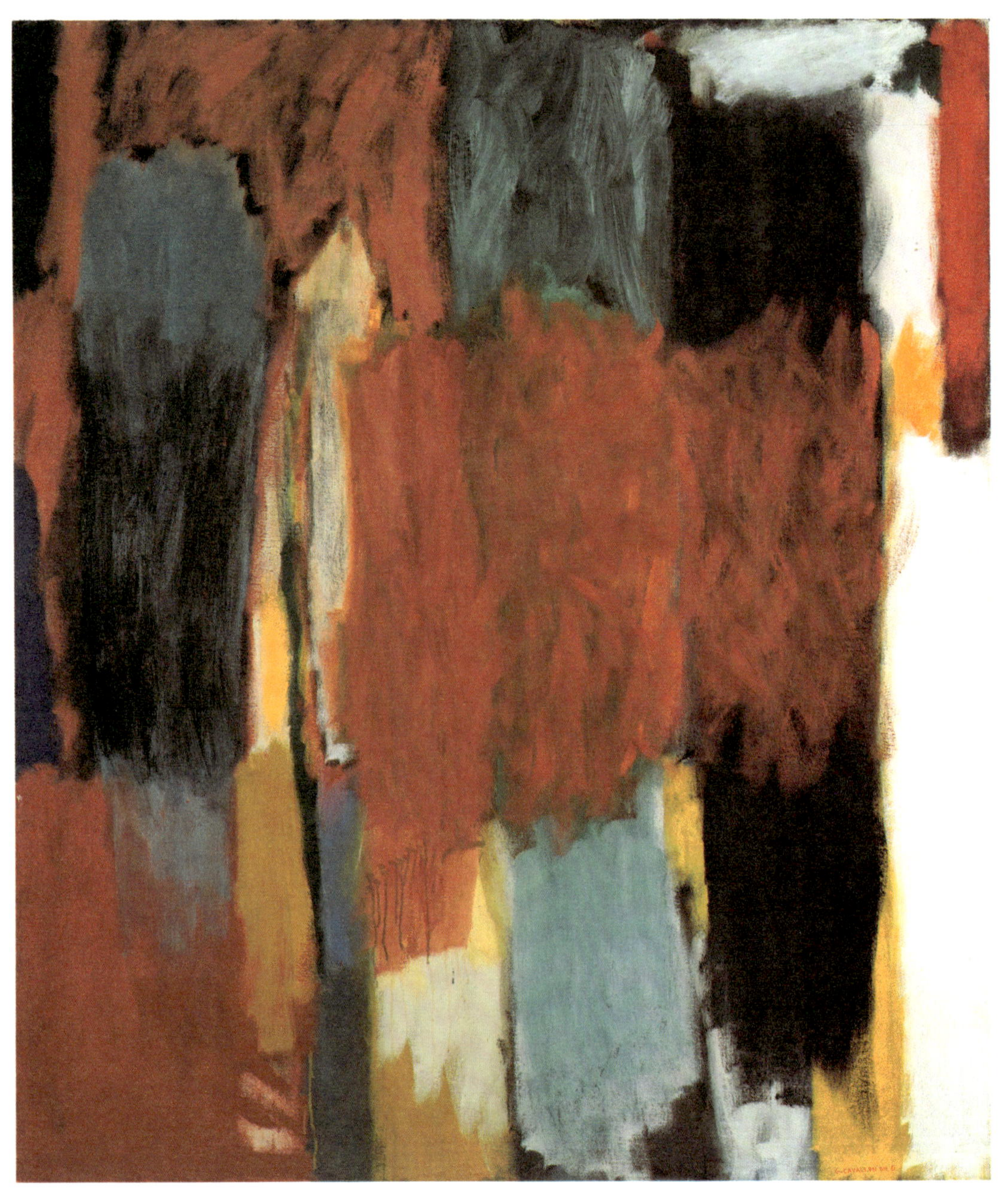

11

GIORGIO CAVALLON (1904–1989)
Untitled, 1961

Oil on canvas, 56 × 48
The Metropolitan Museum of Art; Gift of Lari Stanton, 1986

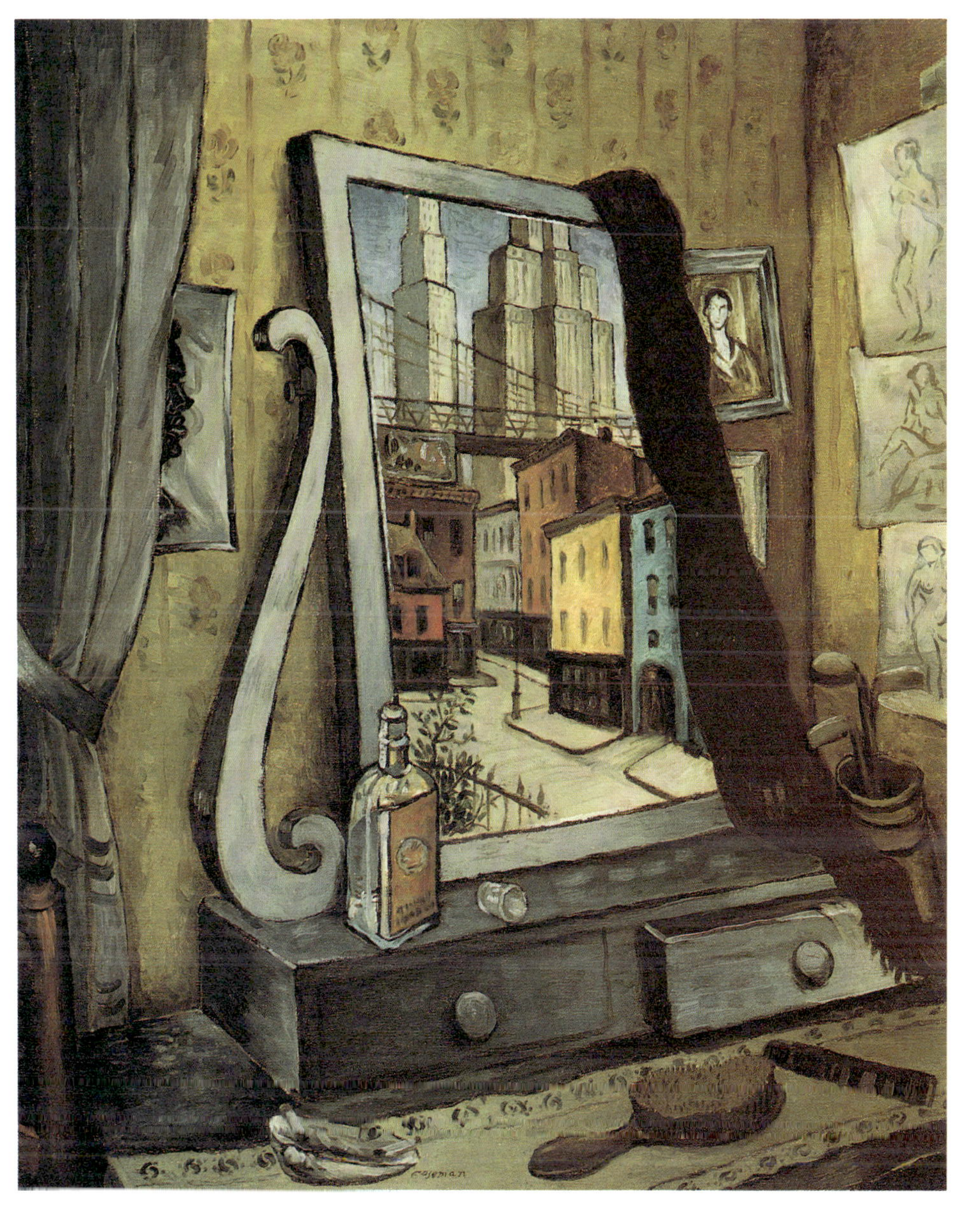

12

GLENN O. COLEMAN (1887–1932)
The Mirror, 1927

Oil on canvas, 30 × 25
Whitney Museum of American Art, New York;
Gift of Gertrude Vanderbilt Whitney

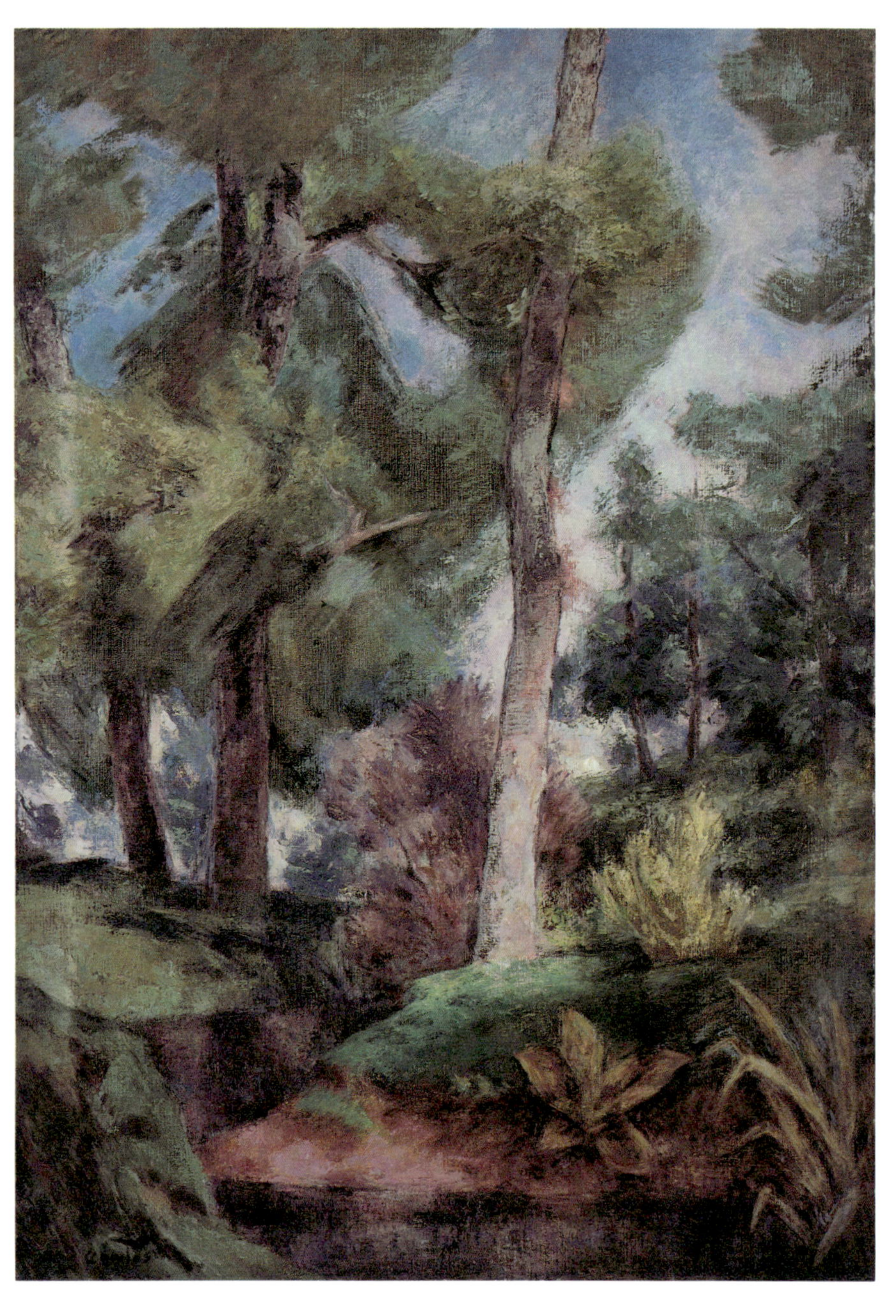

13
RUSSELL COWLES (1887–1979)
Woodland Magic, 1944
Oil on canvas, 39½ × 28
Wichita Art Museum, Wichita, Kansas;
The Roland P. Murdock Collection

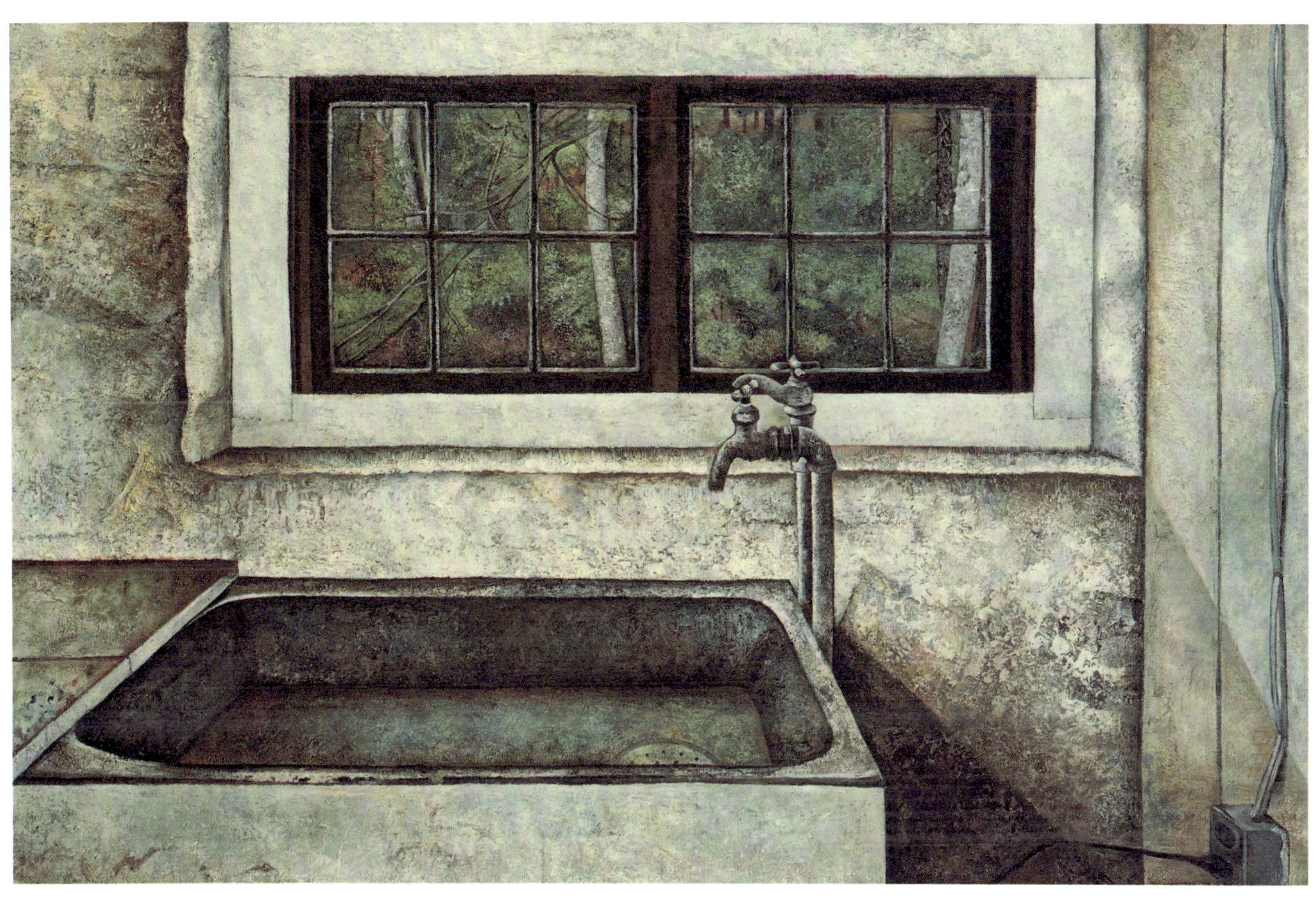

14

SIMON DINNERSTEIN (b. 1943)
Alexander Studio, 1979
Oil on wood panel, 42 × 64
Collection of the Artist

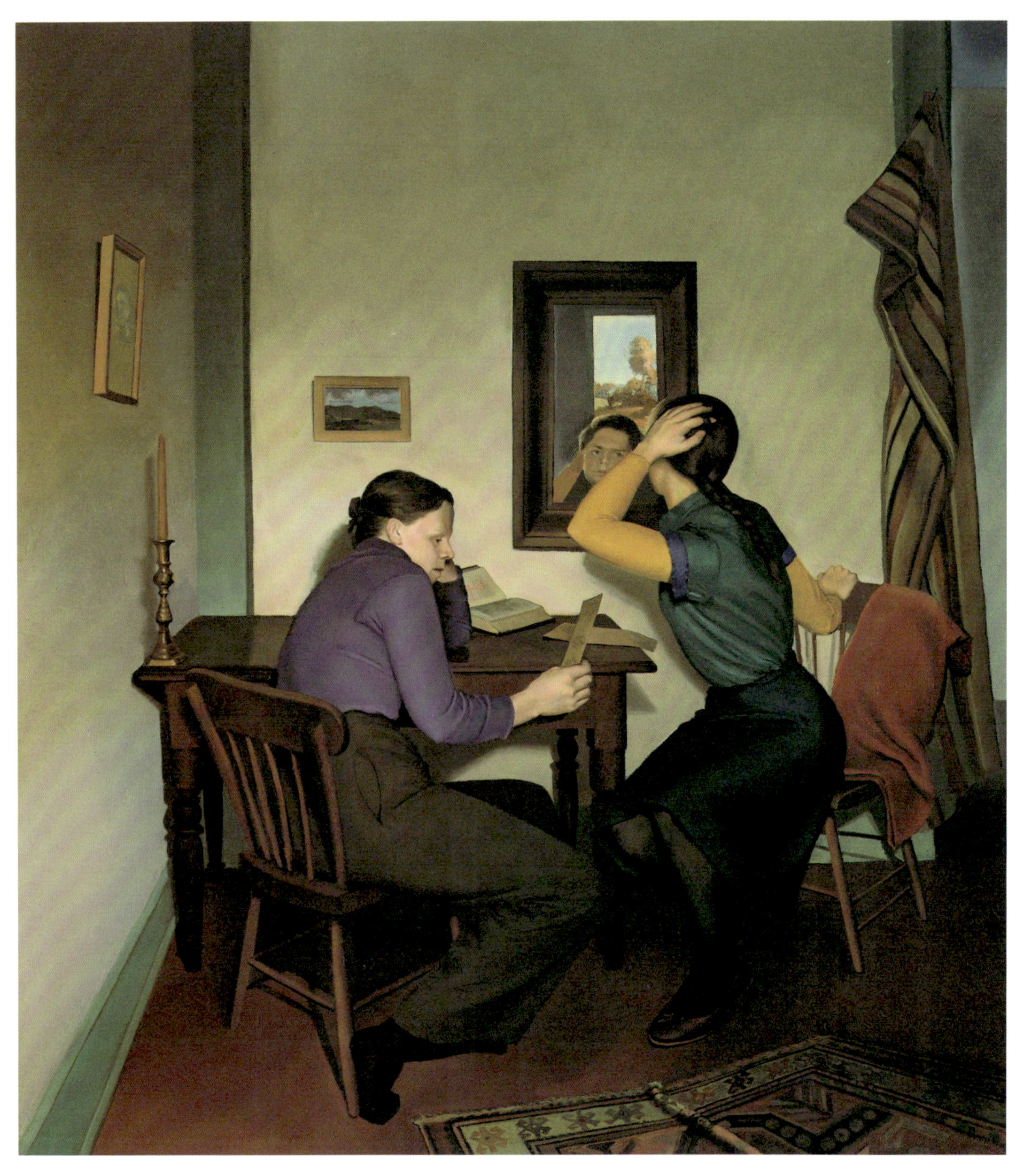

15

JEANNE DUVAL (b. 1956)
Ethereal and Earthbound, 1982

Oil on canvas, 40 × 36
The Metropolitan Museum of Art; Gift of Harvey Kenneth Shepard
and Nancy Massett Shepard, in memory of Edward Massett, 1983

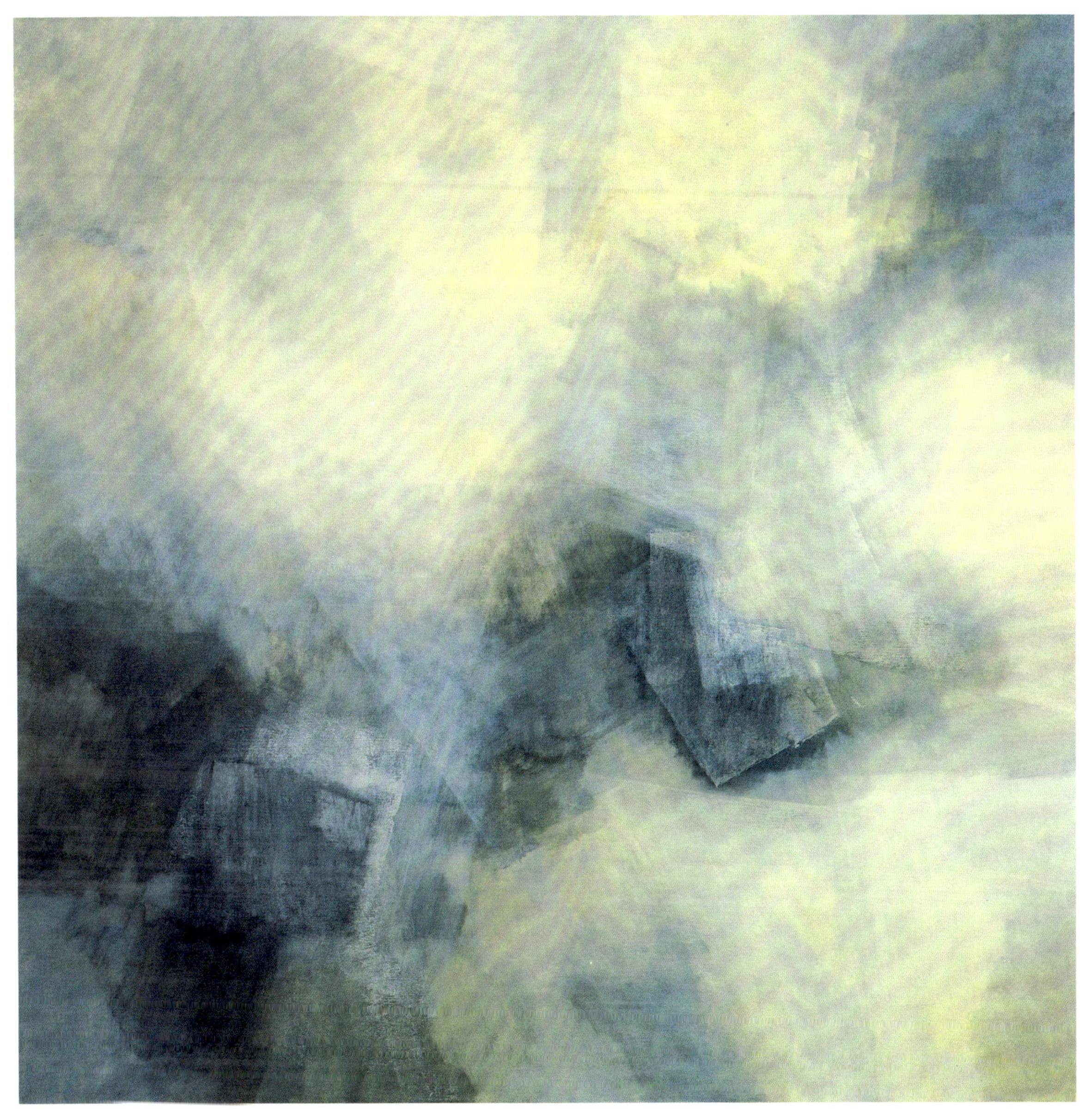

16

ROBERT ESHOO (b. 1926)
Refraction II, 1959–60
Oil on canvas, 70⅛ × 70⅛
The Currier Gallery of Art, Manchester, New Hampshire;
Museum purchase: gift of an anonymous donor through
the American Federation of Arts

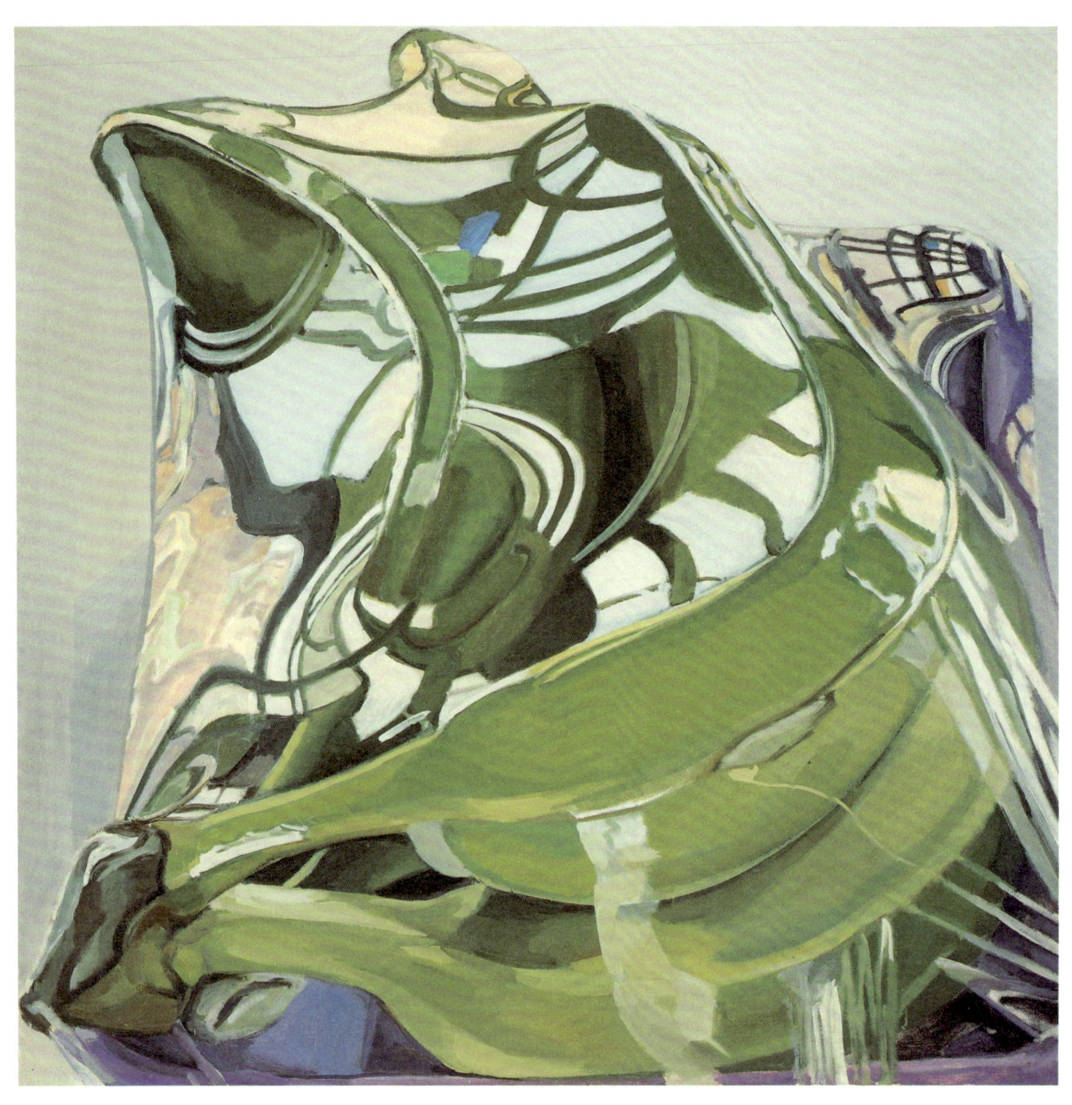

17
JANET FISH (b. 1938)
Plantains in a Box, 1969
Oil on canvas, 44 × 44
Collection of the Artist

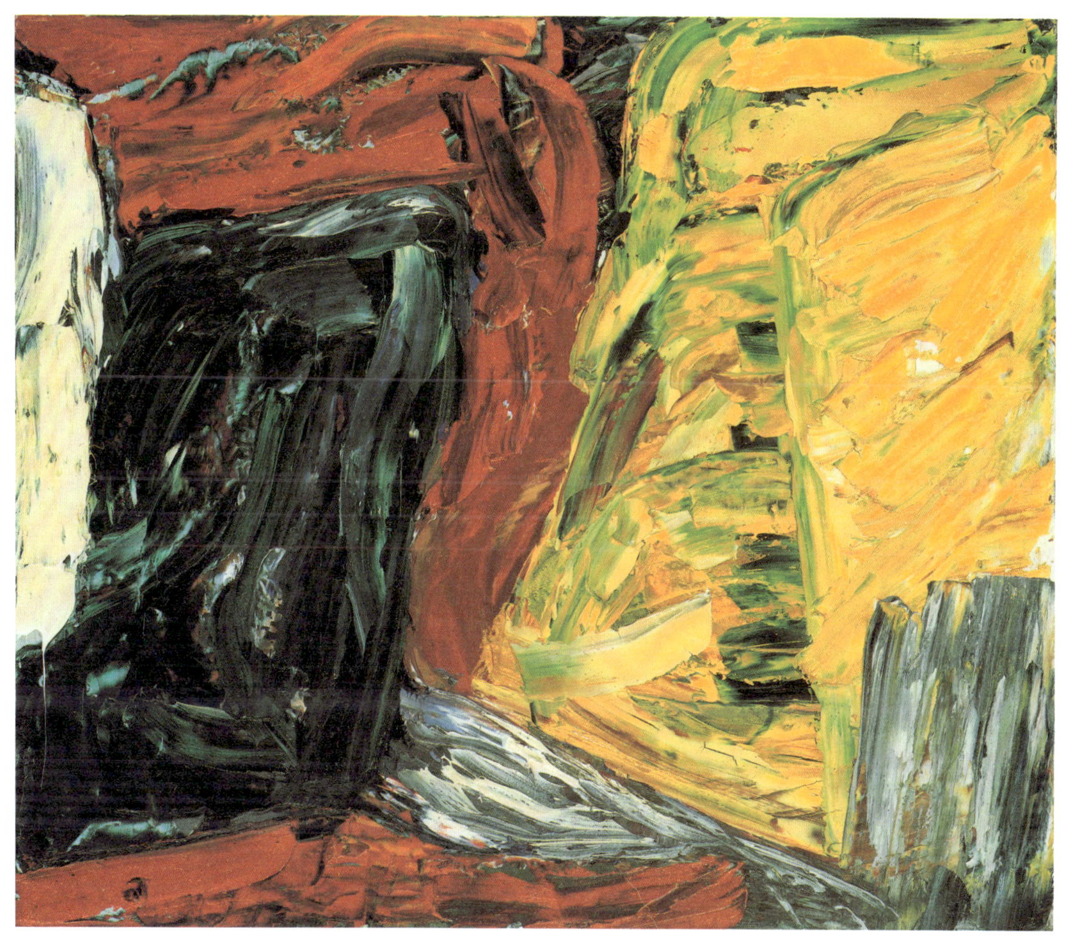

18

LOUISE FISHMAN (b. 1939)
MacDowell #9, 1980
Oil on linen, 19 × 22
Courtesy of the Artist and Robert Miller Gallery, New York

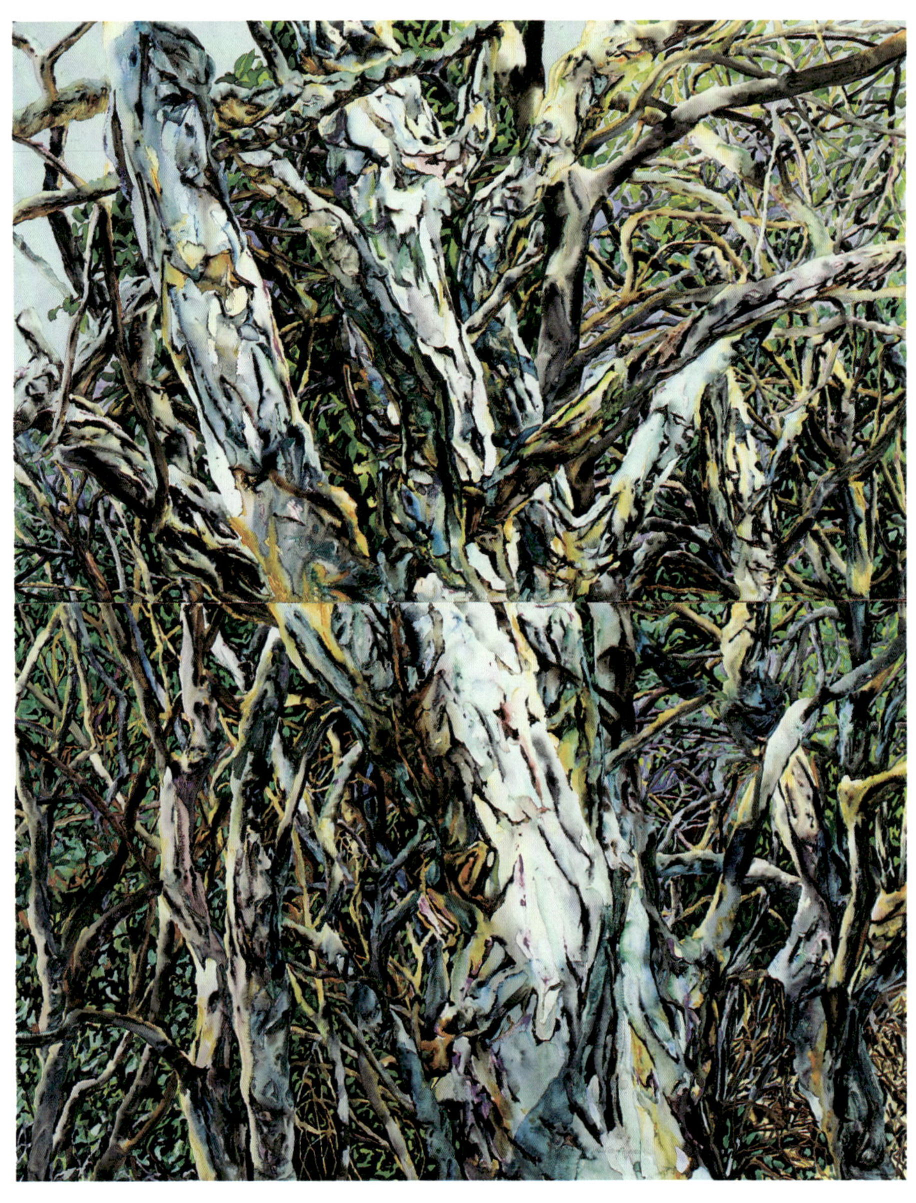

19

PATRICIA TOBACCO FORRESTER (b. 1940)

In Ann's Meadow, 1980

Watercolor, 50 × 40

Collection of the Artist

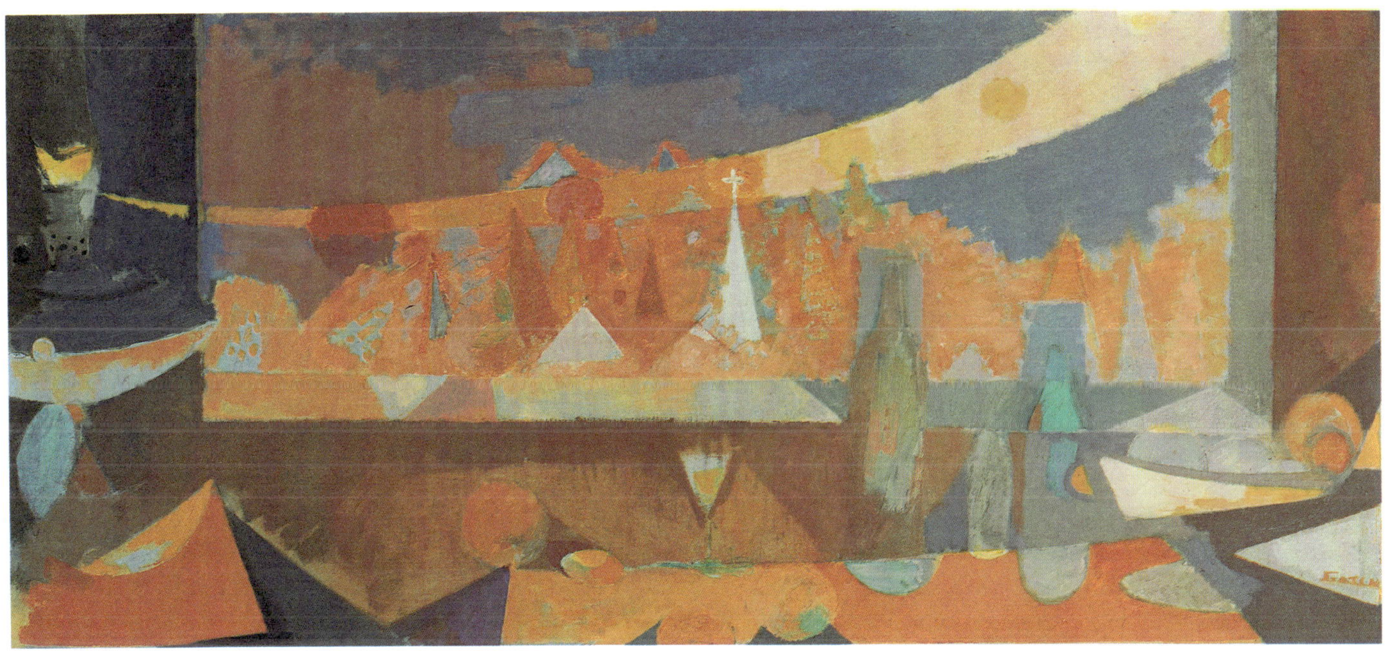

20

LEE GATCH (1902–1968)

The Path of the Sun, 1948–49

Oil on canvas, 21 × 47½

Neuberger Museum of Art, Purchase College,
State University of New York; Gift of Roy R. Neuberger

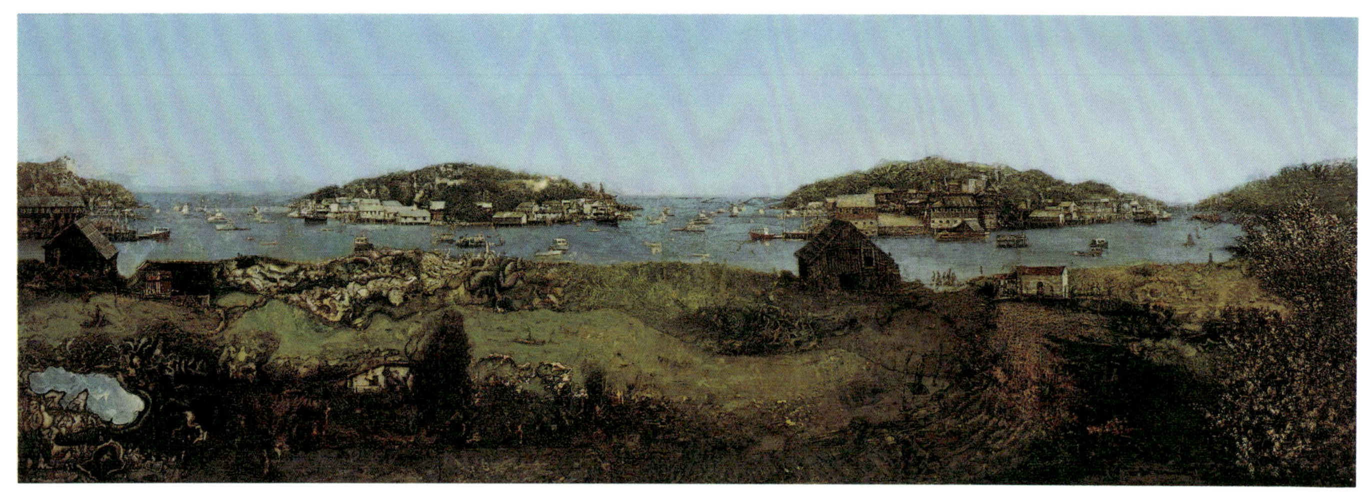

21

GREGORY GILLESPIE (b. 1936)
Landscape with Islands and Sky, 1979

Oil on particle board, 12⅛ × 35⅞
The Metropolitan Museum of Art;
Gift of the family of Charles Wilmers, in his honor, 1982

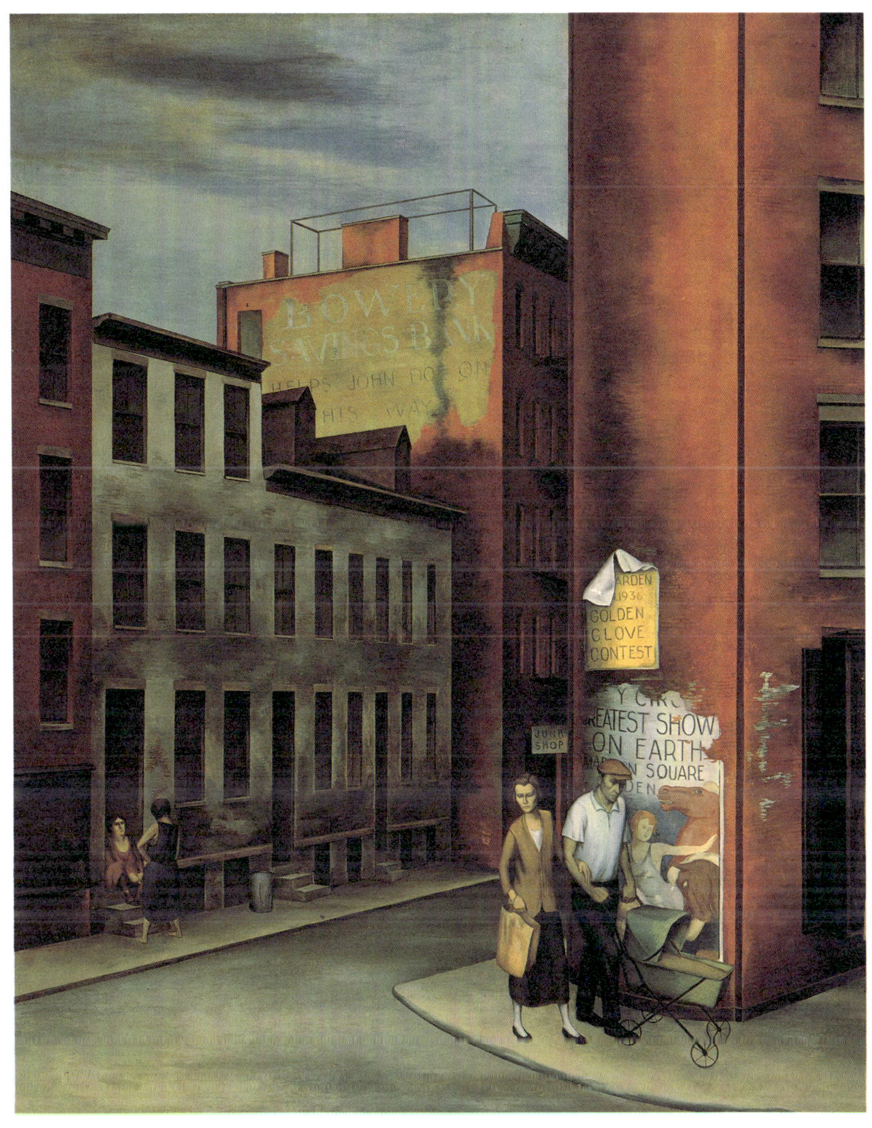

22

O. LOUIS GUGLIELMI (1906–1956)
View in Chambers Street, 1936

Oil on canvas, 30 × 24
The Newark Museum; Allocated by the WPA Federal Art Project, 1943

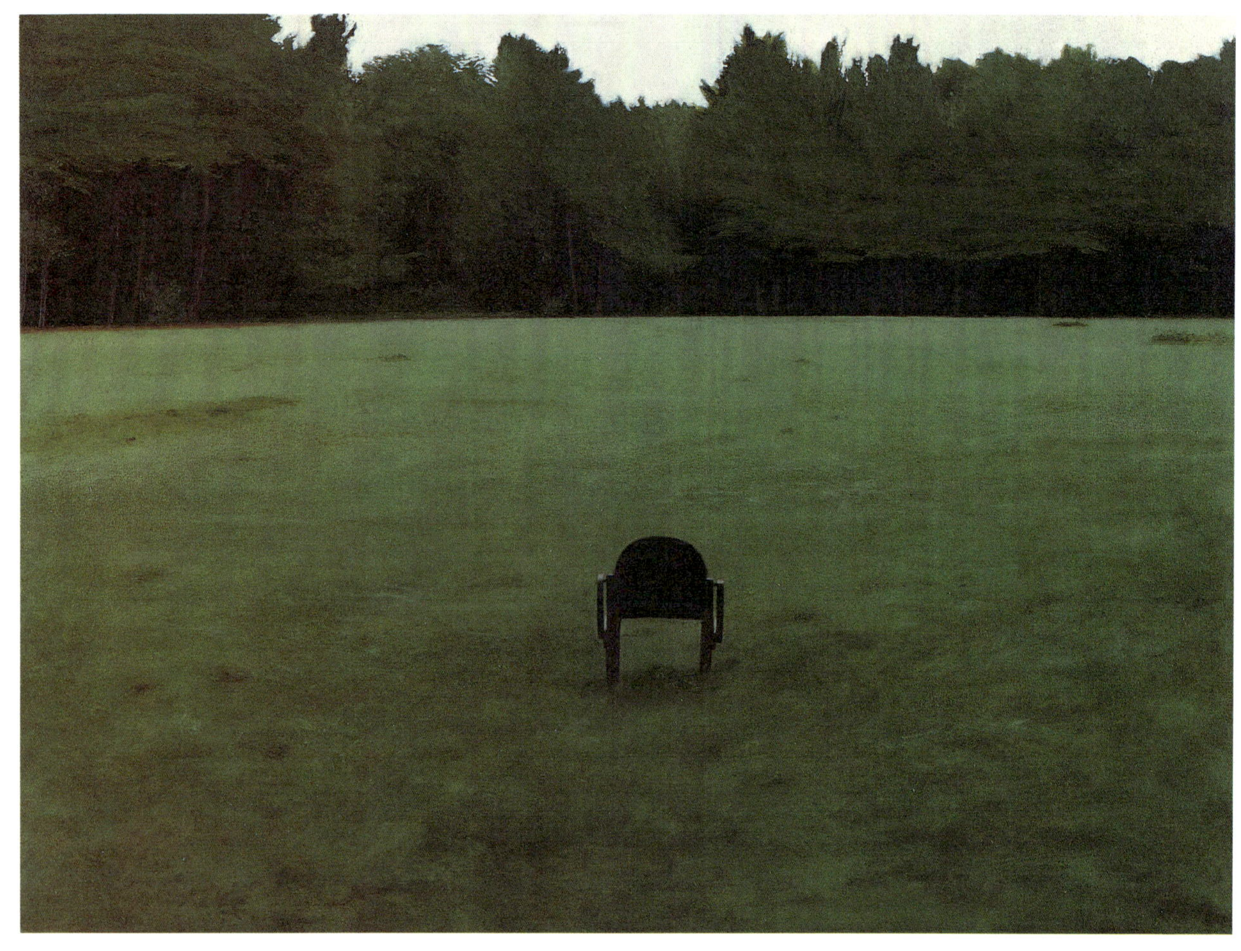

23
SUSAN HAMBLETON (b. 1940)
Thinking of You, 1989
Oil on canvas, 39½ × 53¼
Collection of Dr. and Mrs. William Fritz

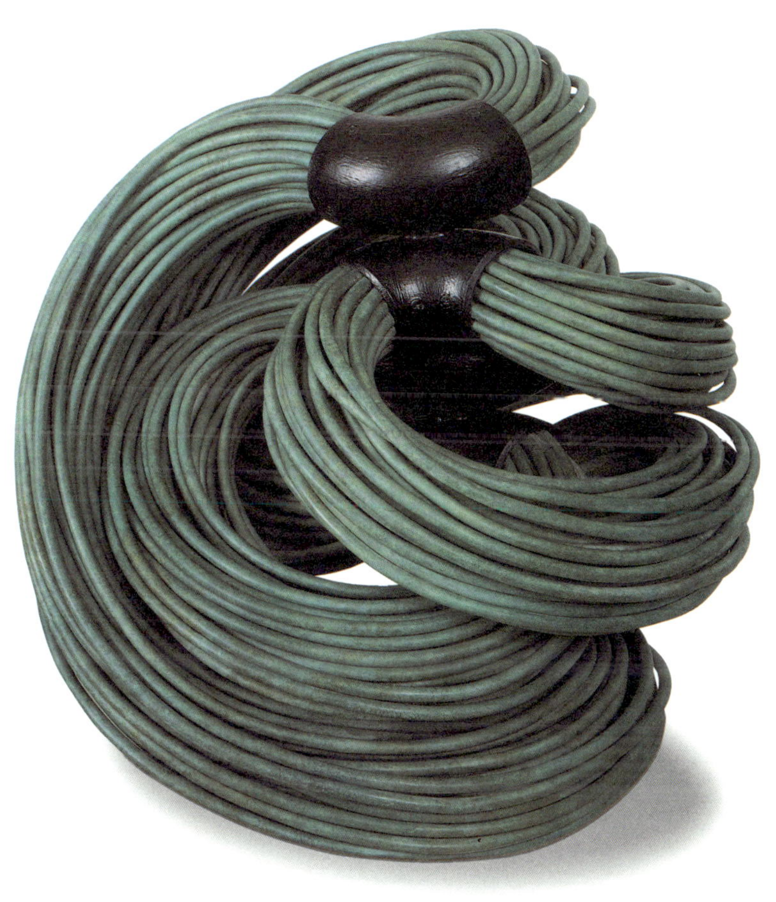

24
CAROL HEPPER (b. 1953)
Spinal Tap II, 1992
Copper, steel, 27 × 27 × 33
Private Collection

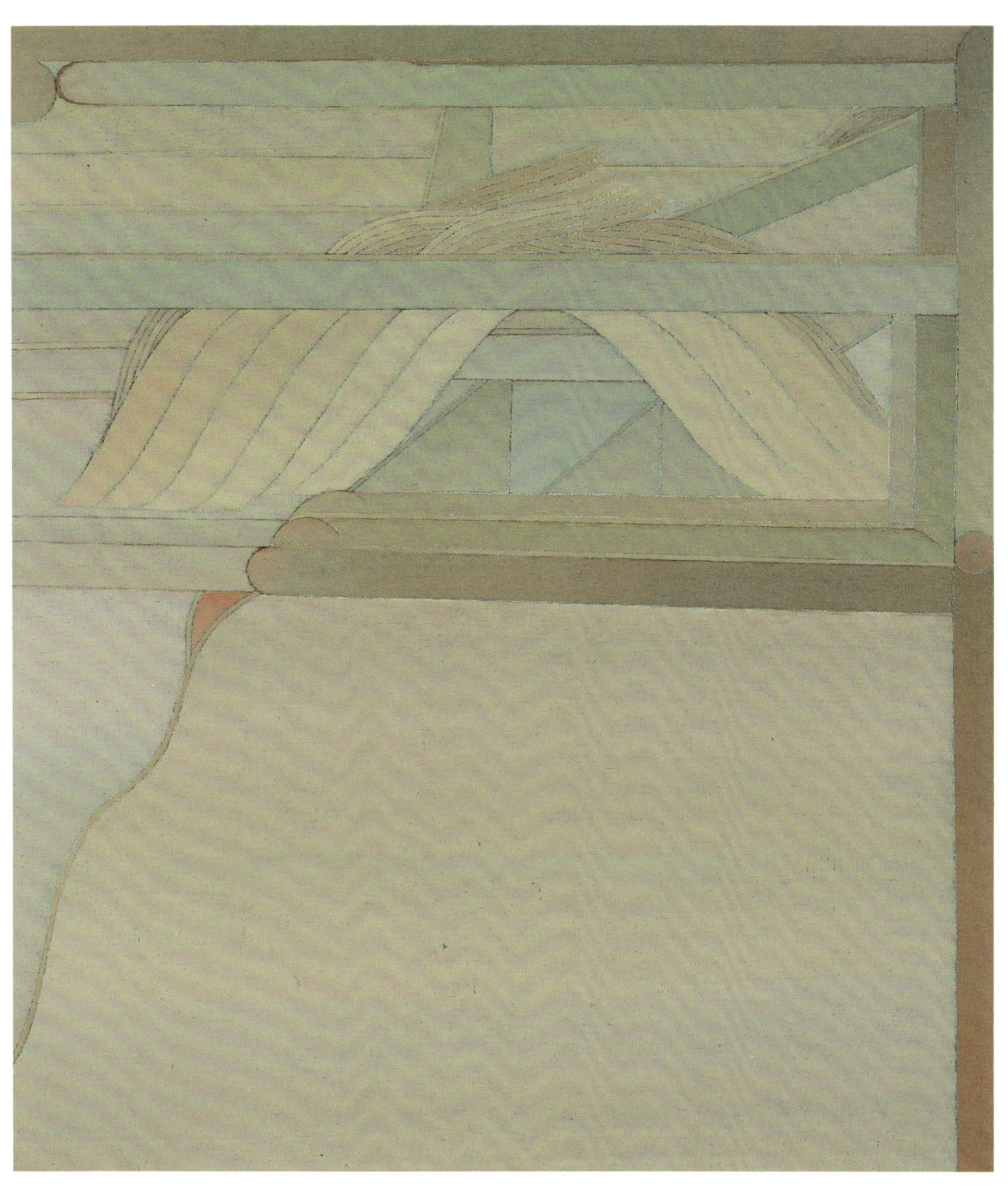

25
MIYOKO ITO (1918–1983)
Untitled, about 1975
Oil on canvas, 46 × 40
Courtesy Phyllis Kind Gallery, New York / Chicago

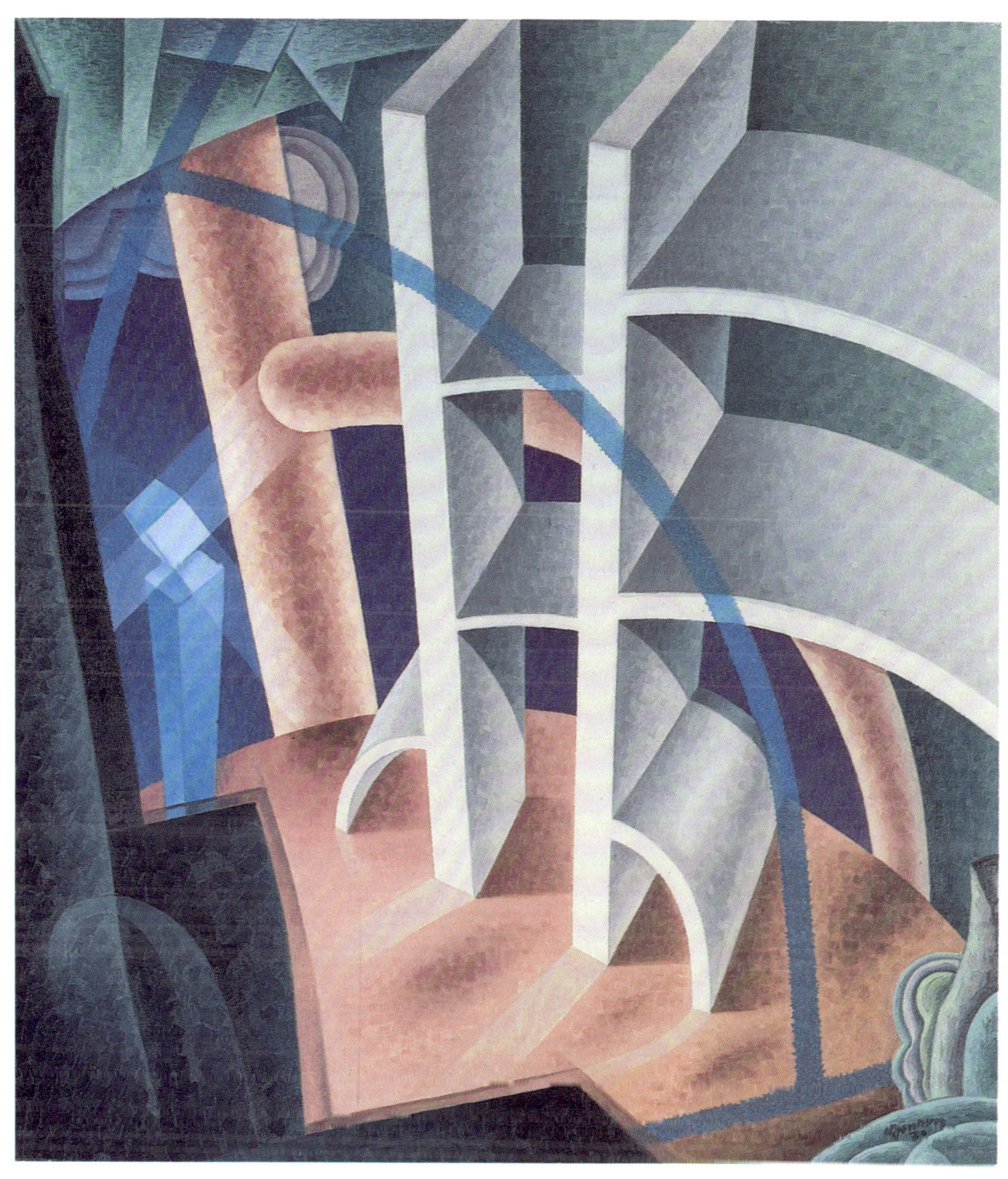

26

RAYMOND JONSON (1891–1982)

Variations on a Rhythm – H, 1931

Oil on canvas, 33⅛ × 29

National Museum of American Art, Smithsonian Institution;
Gift of Patricia and Phillip Frost

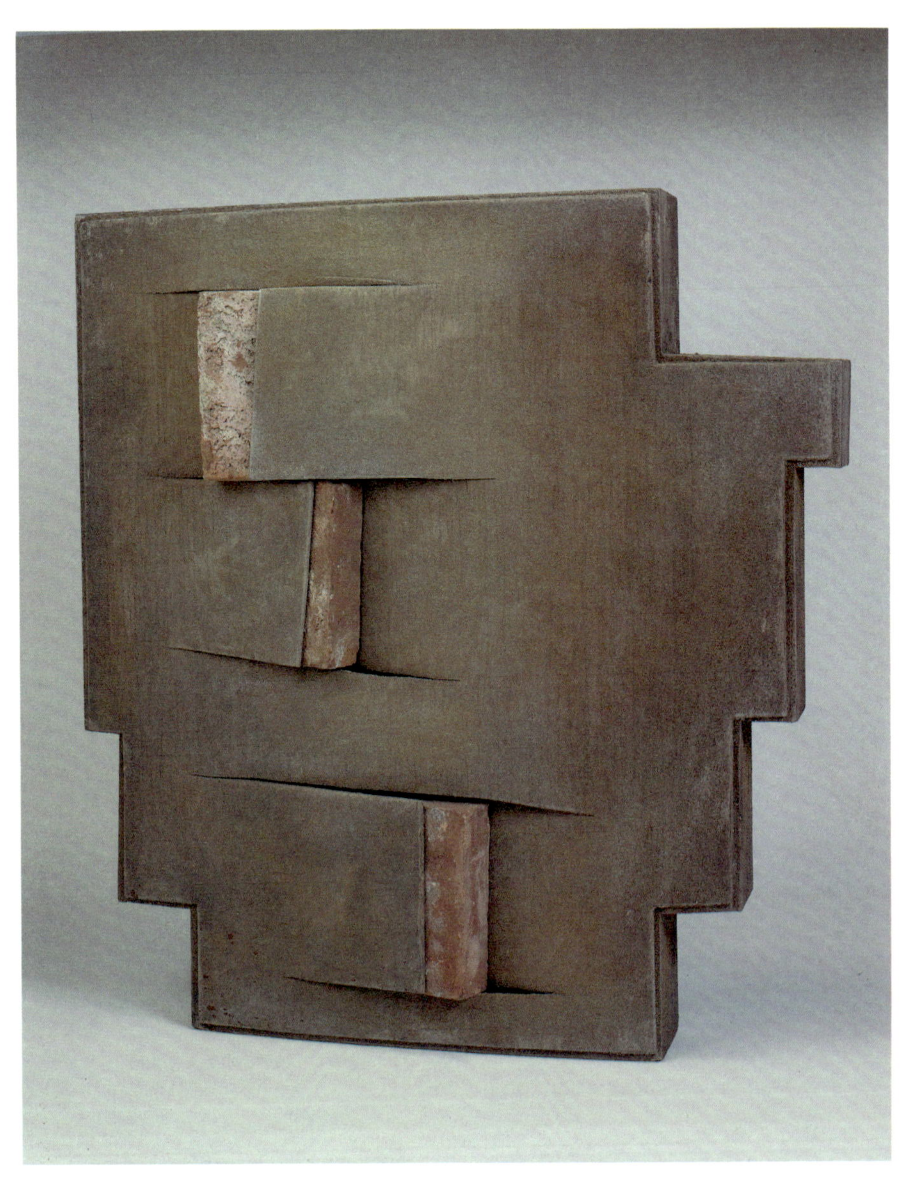

27
HARRY E. LEIGH (b. 1931)
Untitled, 1987
Wood, brick, acrylic paint, sand,
mixed materials, 36½ × 35 × 8
Collection of the Artist

28

GLENN LIGON (b. 1960)

Untitled, 1992

Series of four etchings, each 25 × 17¼

Courtesy Glenn Ligon and Max Protetch Gallery, New York

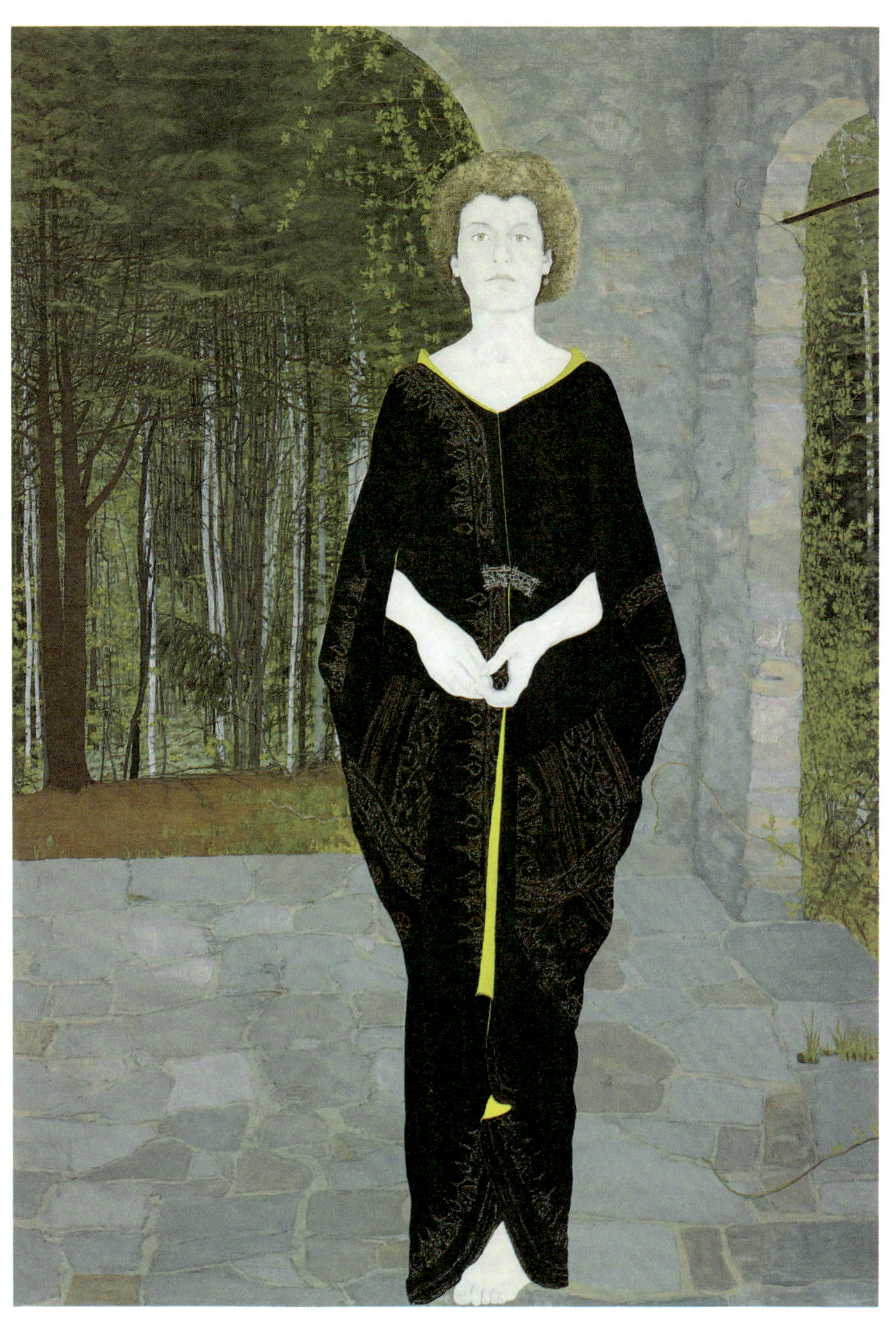

29

MARCIA MARCUS (b. 1928)

Self-Portrait at MacDowell Colony, New Hampshire, 1969

Oil on canvas, 76 × 53

Phoenix Art Museum; Gift of American Academy of Arts and Letters, Childe Hassam Fund

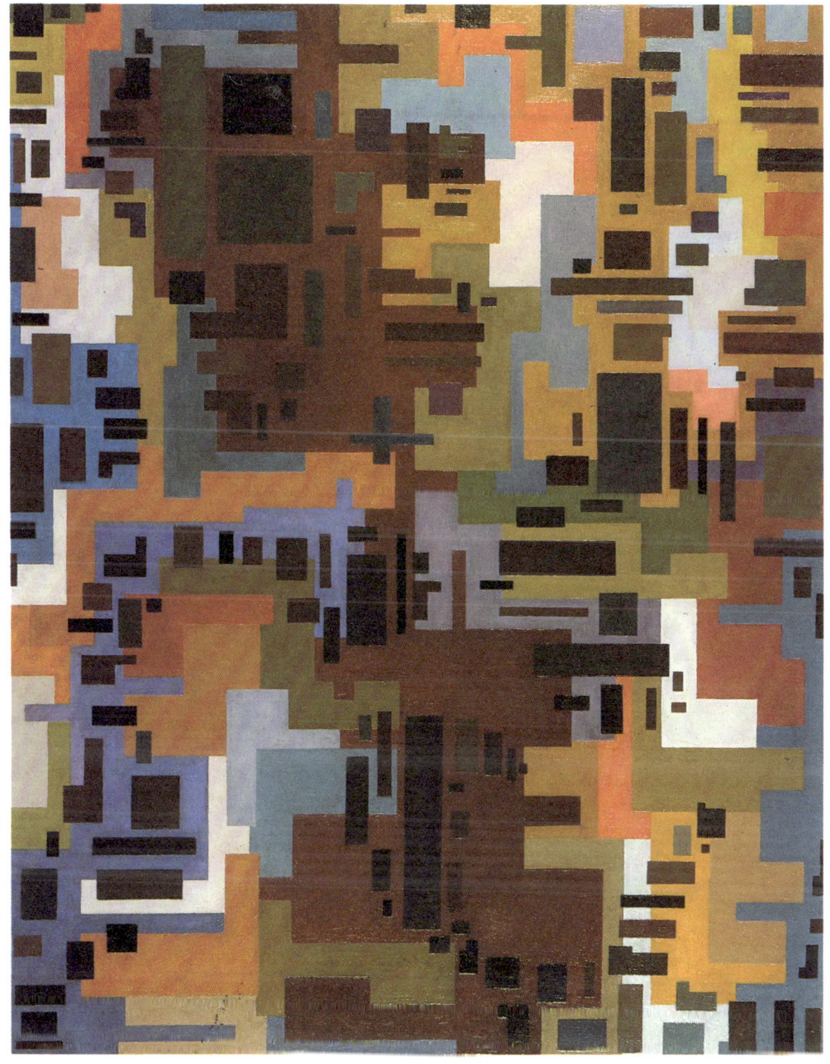

30

ALICE TRUMBULL MASON (1904–1971)

L'Hasard, 1948

Oil on masonite, 36½ × 28⅜

Museum of Art, Rhode Island School of Design, Providence;

Helen M. Danforth Fund

Exhibited at The Currier Gallery of Art only

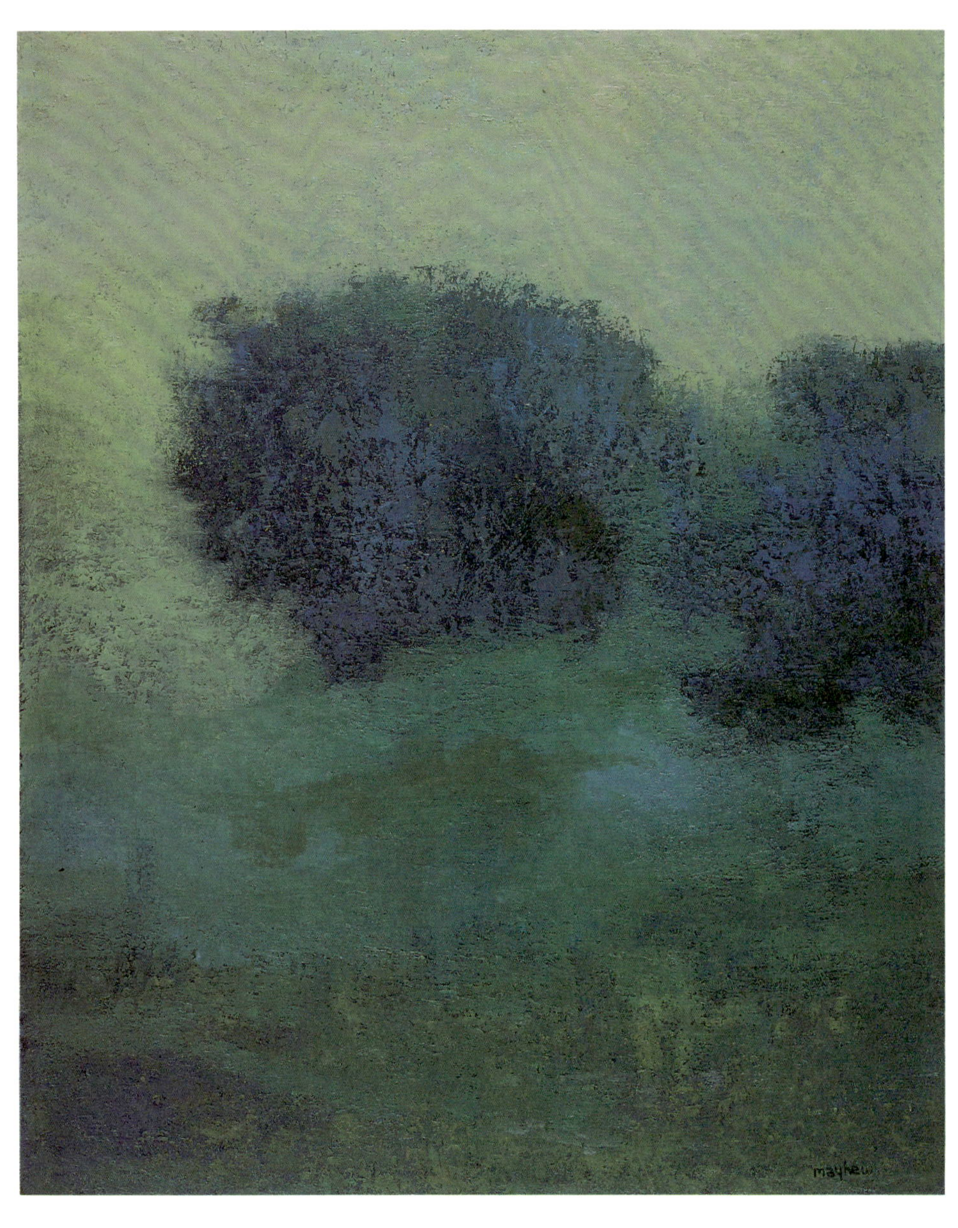

31

RICHARD MAYHEW (b. 1934)

MacDowell Summer, about 1958

Oil on canvas, 30 × 24

Collection of William Nathaniel Banks

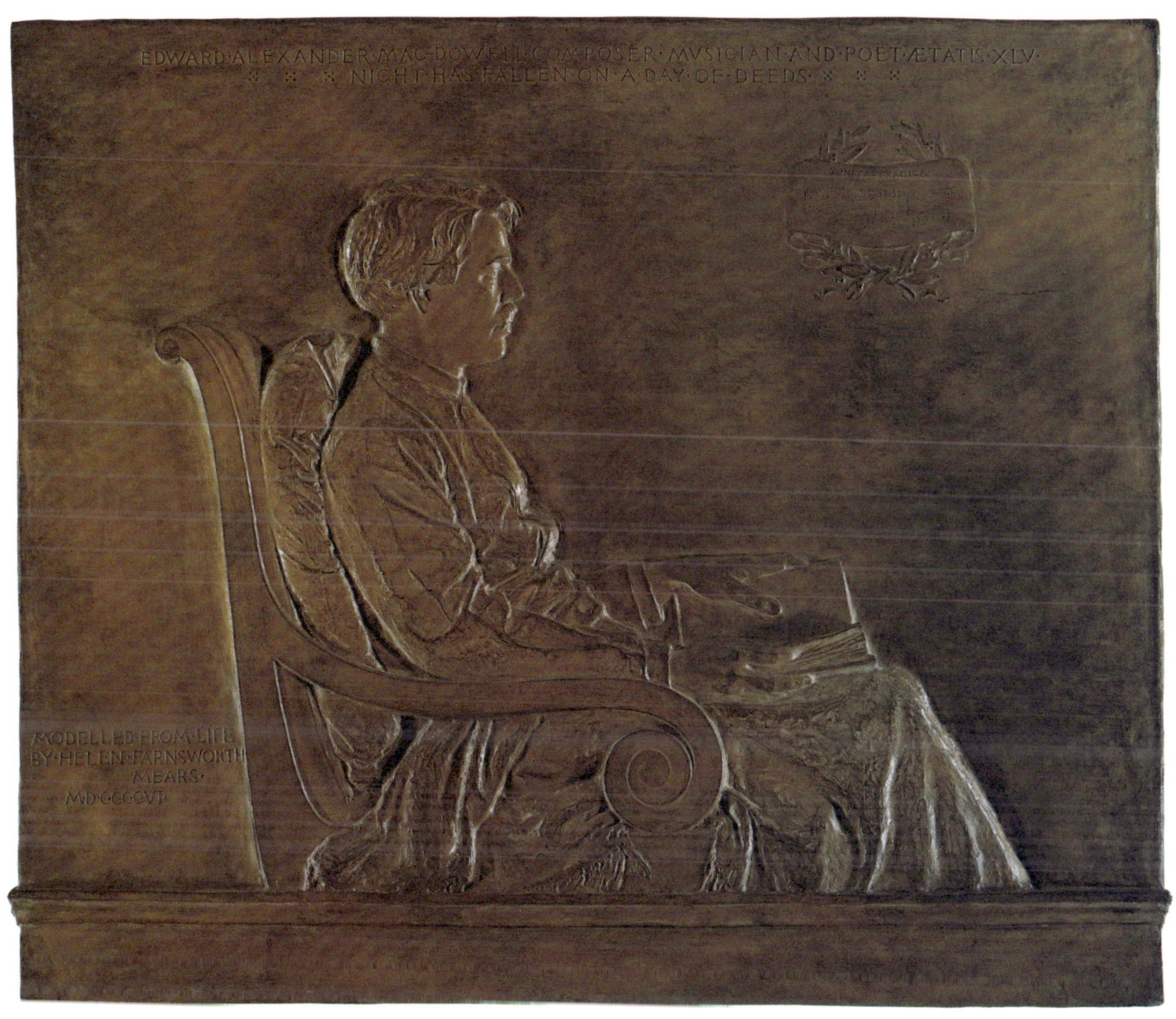

32

HELEN FARNSWORTH MEARS (1871–1916)
Edward Alexander MacDowell, 1906

Bronze, $33\frac{1}{4} \times 39\frac{7}{8}$
The Metropolitan Museum of Art; Gift of Alice G. Chapman, 1909

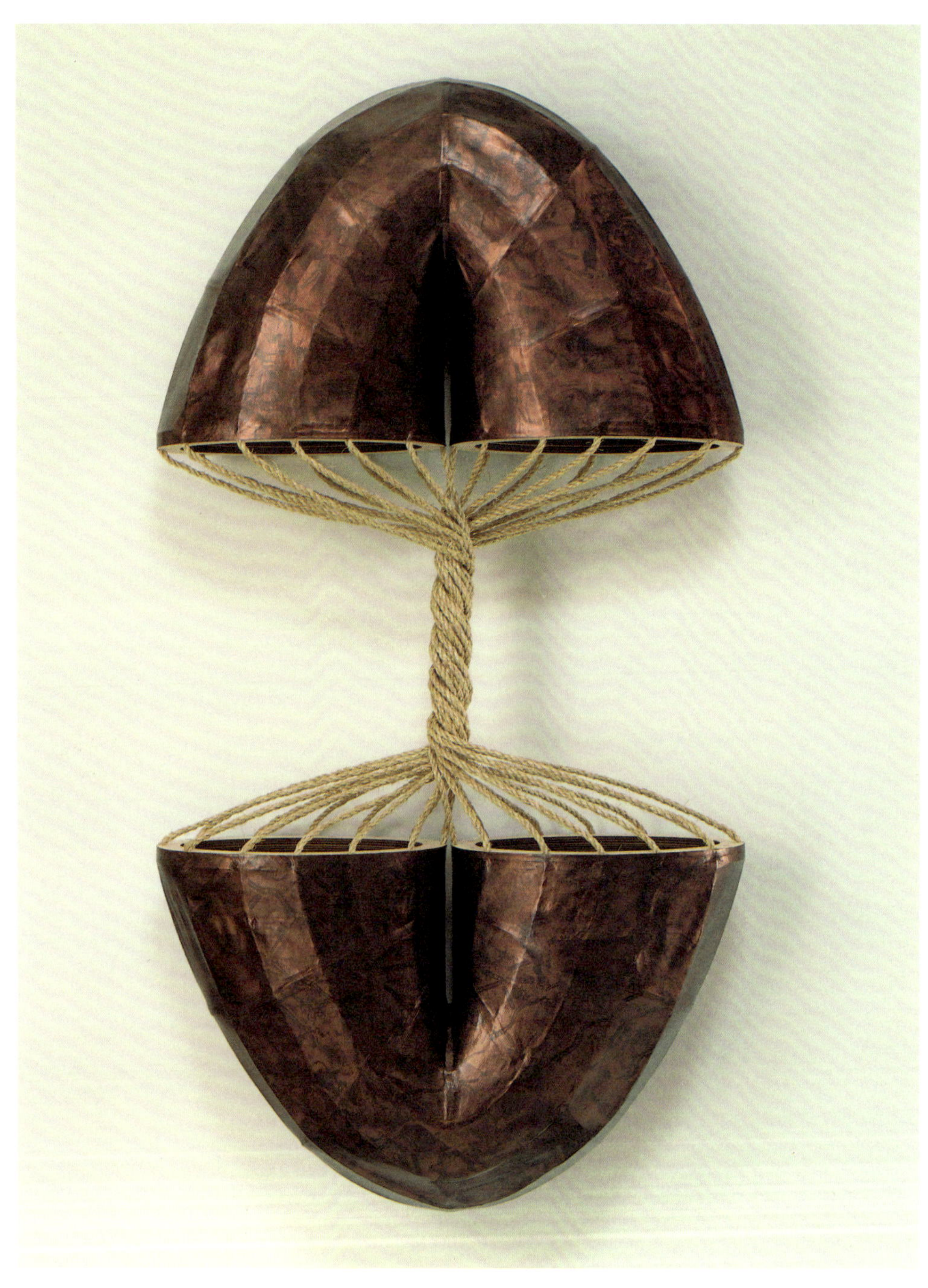

33
JOHN NEWMAN (b. 1952)
Spin Off (copper version), 1992
Rope, wood, kozo fiber coated with metallic foil, 55 × 29 × 10
Courtesy Tyler Graphics Ltd., Mount Kisco,
New York, and Jason McCoy, Inc., New York

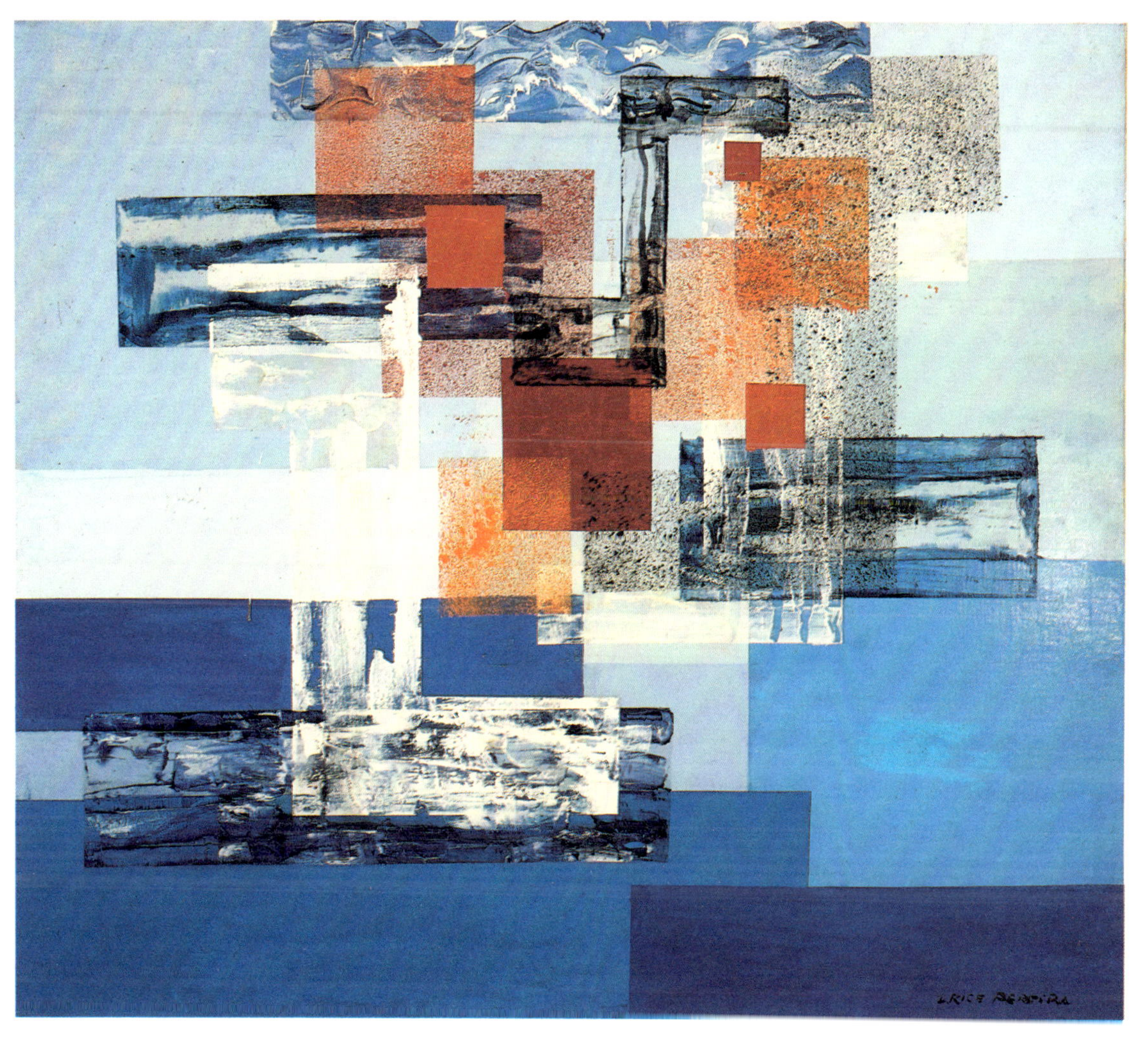

34
IRENE RICE PEREIRA (1902–1971)
Core of Substance, 1956
Oil on canvas, 44 × 50
Courtesy Andre Zarre Gallery, New York

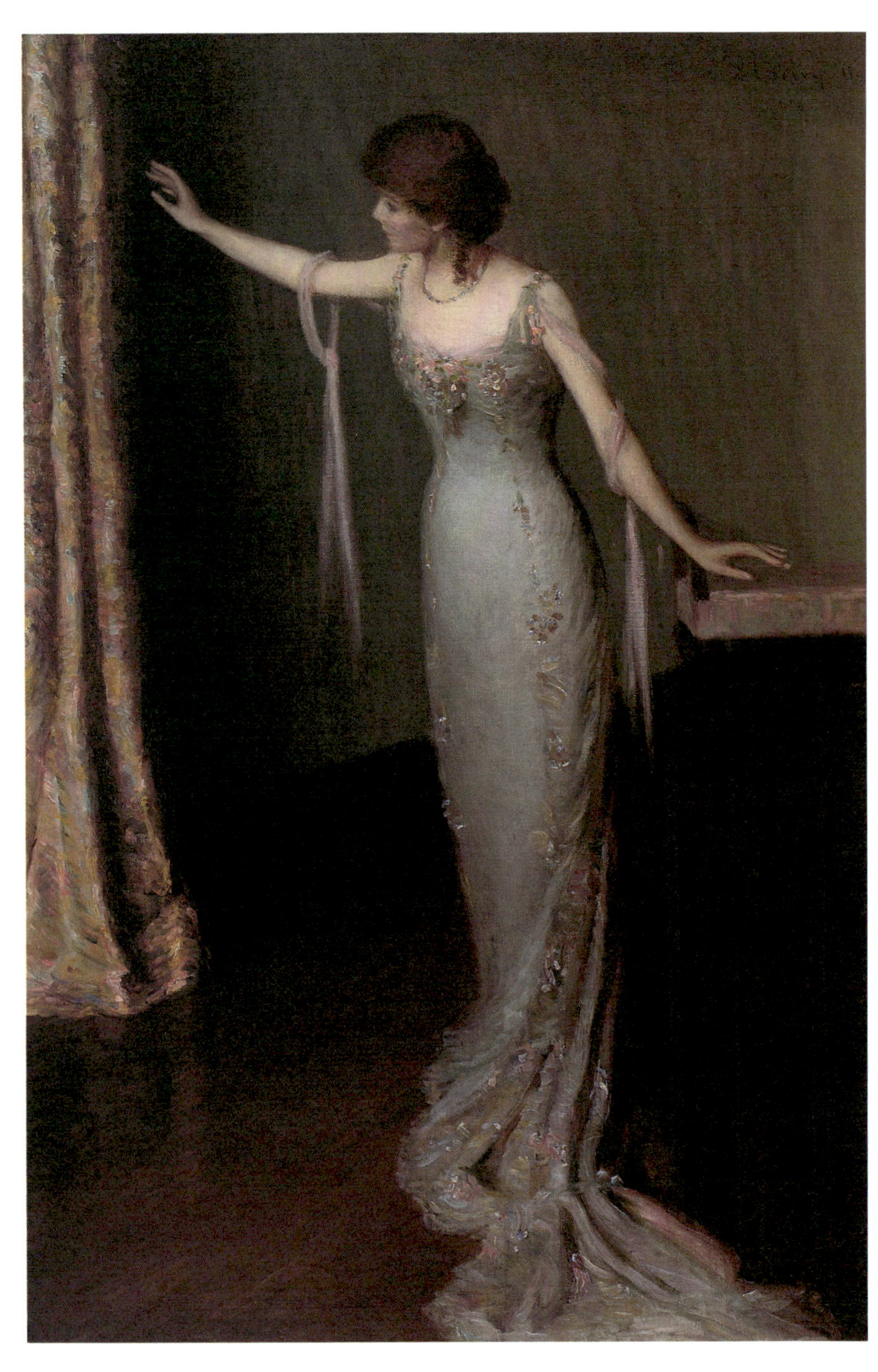

35
LILLA CABOT PERRY (1848–1933)
Lady in an Evening Dress (Renée), 1911
Oil on canvas, 36 × 24
The National Museum of Women in the Arts;
Gift of Wallace and Wilhelmina Holladay

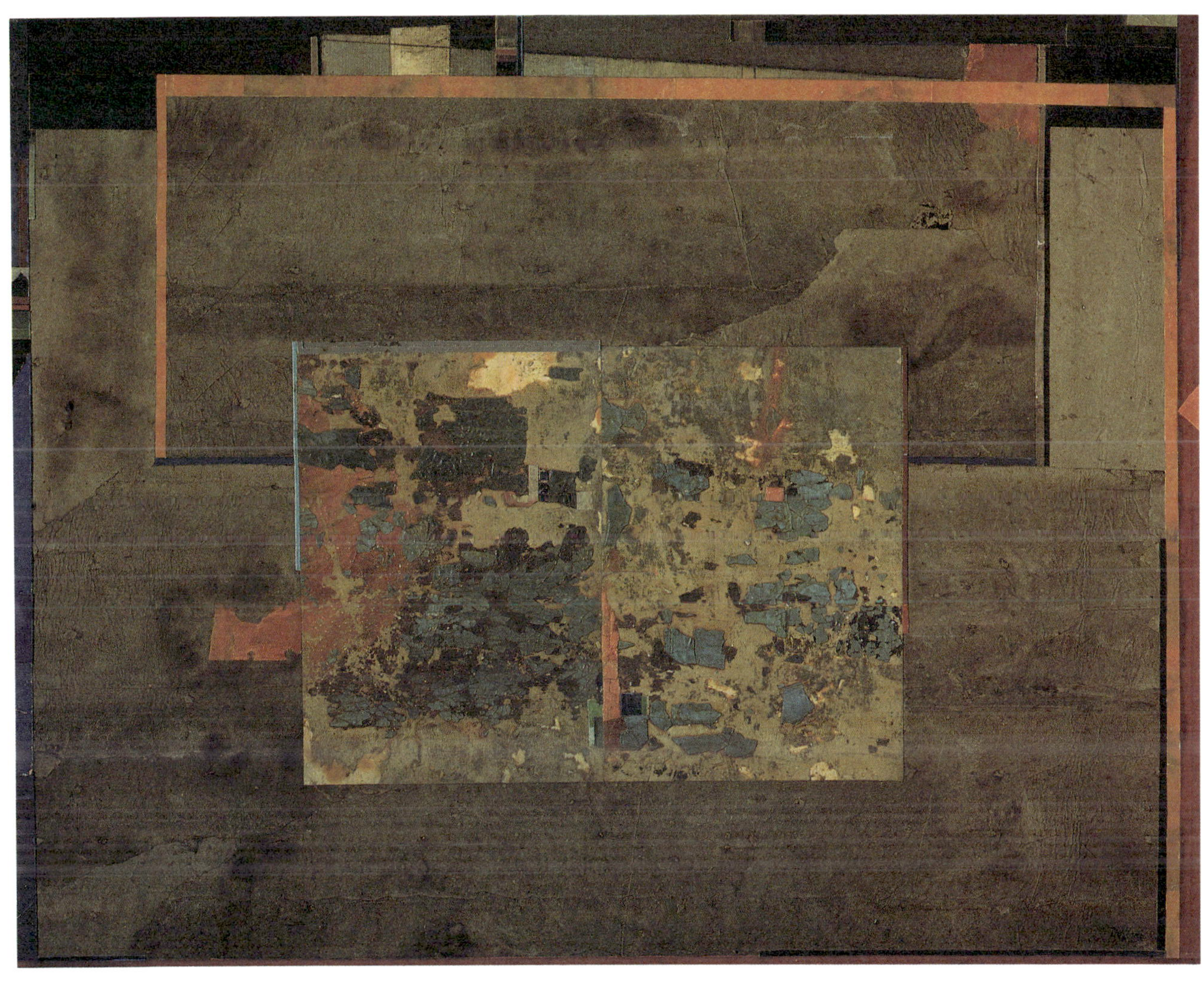

36
PAUL POLLARO (b. 1921)
Temple VI, 1988
Mixed media collage on canvas, 48¼ × 61¾
Private Collection

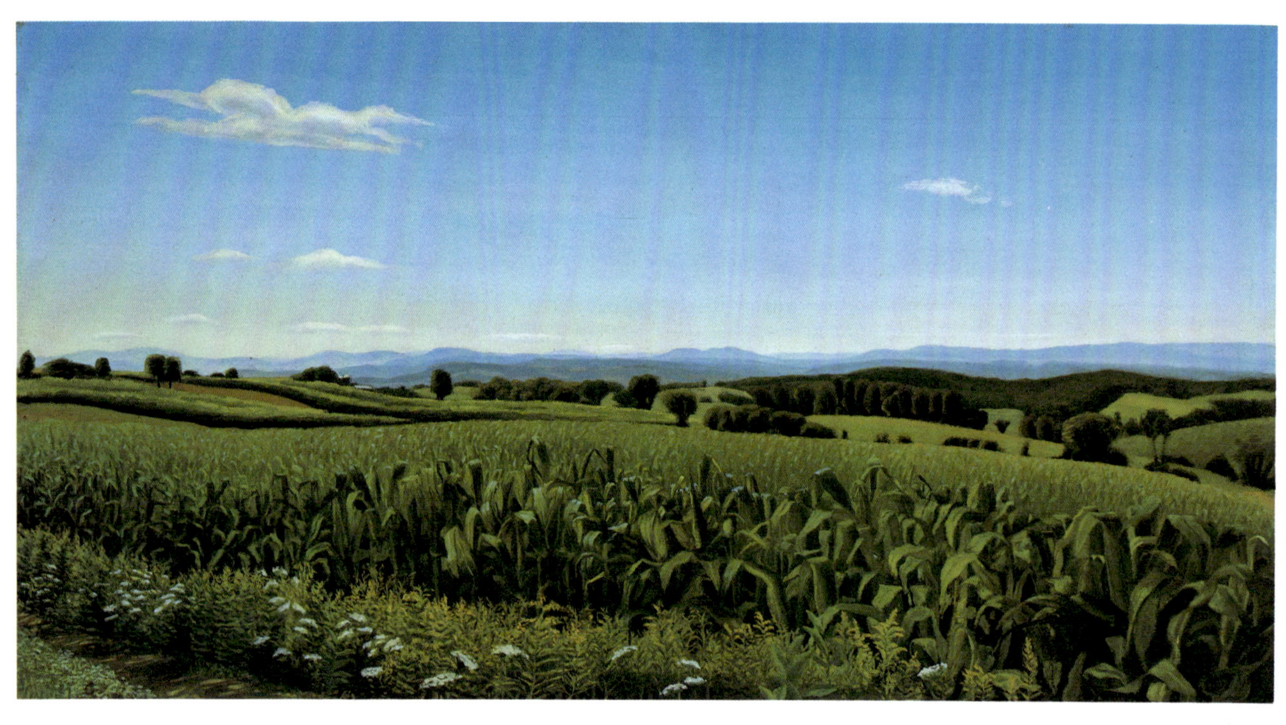

37
MARJORIE PORTNOW (b. 1942)
Cambridge Corn, 1981
Oil on canvas, 16 × 30
The Metropolitan Museum of Art;
Gift of Dr. and Mrs. Robert E. Carroll, 1983

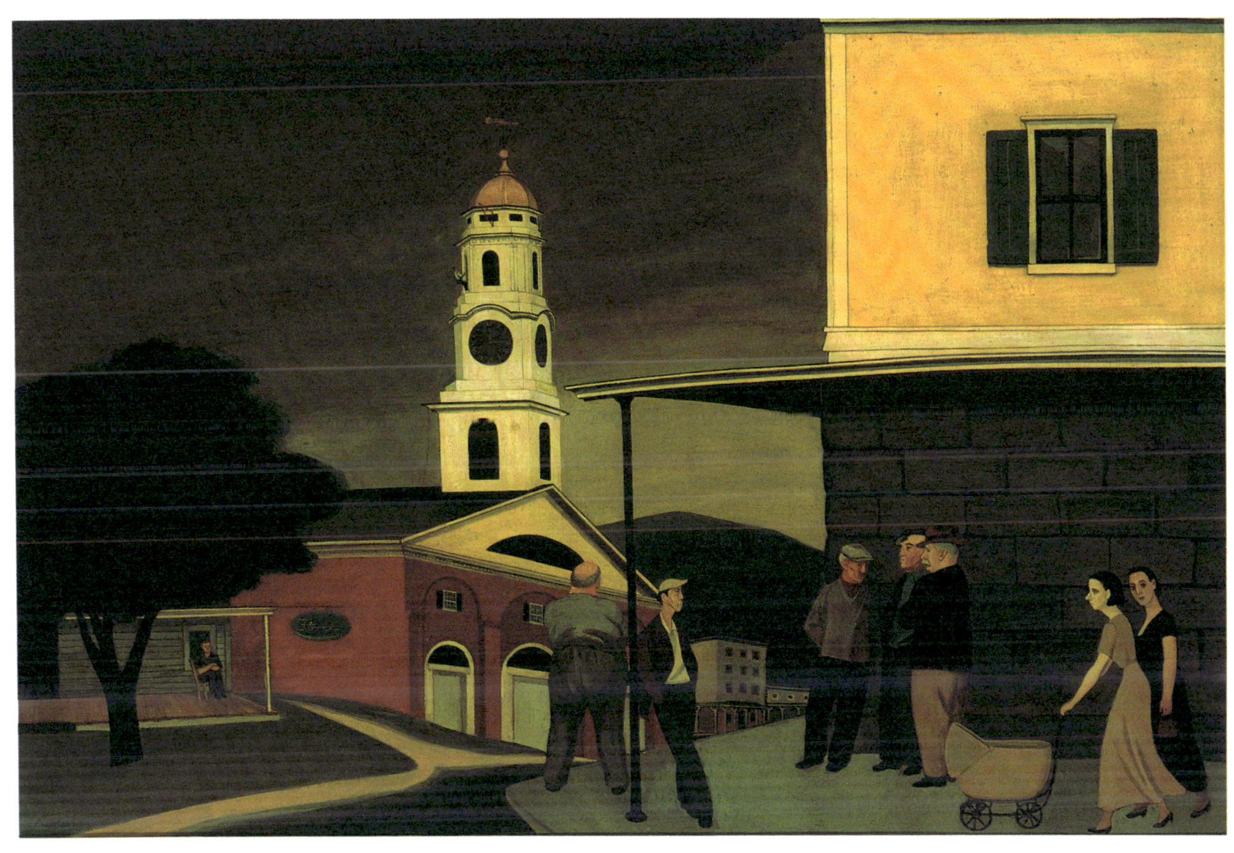

38

GREGORIO PRESTOPINO (1907–1984)
Main Street, Peterborough, 1935

Egg tempera on masonite, 20 × 30
Collection of Mrs. Elizabeth D. Prestopino

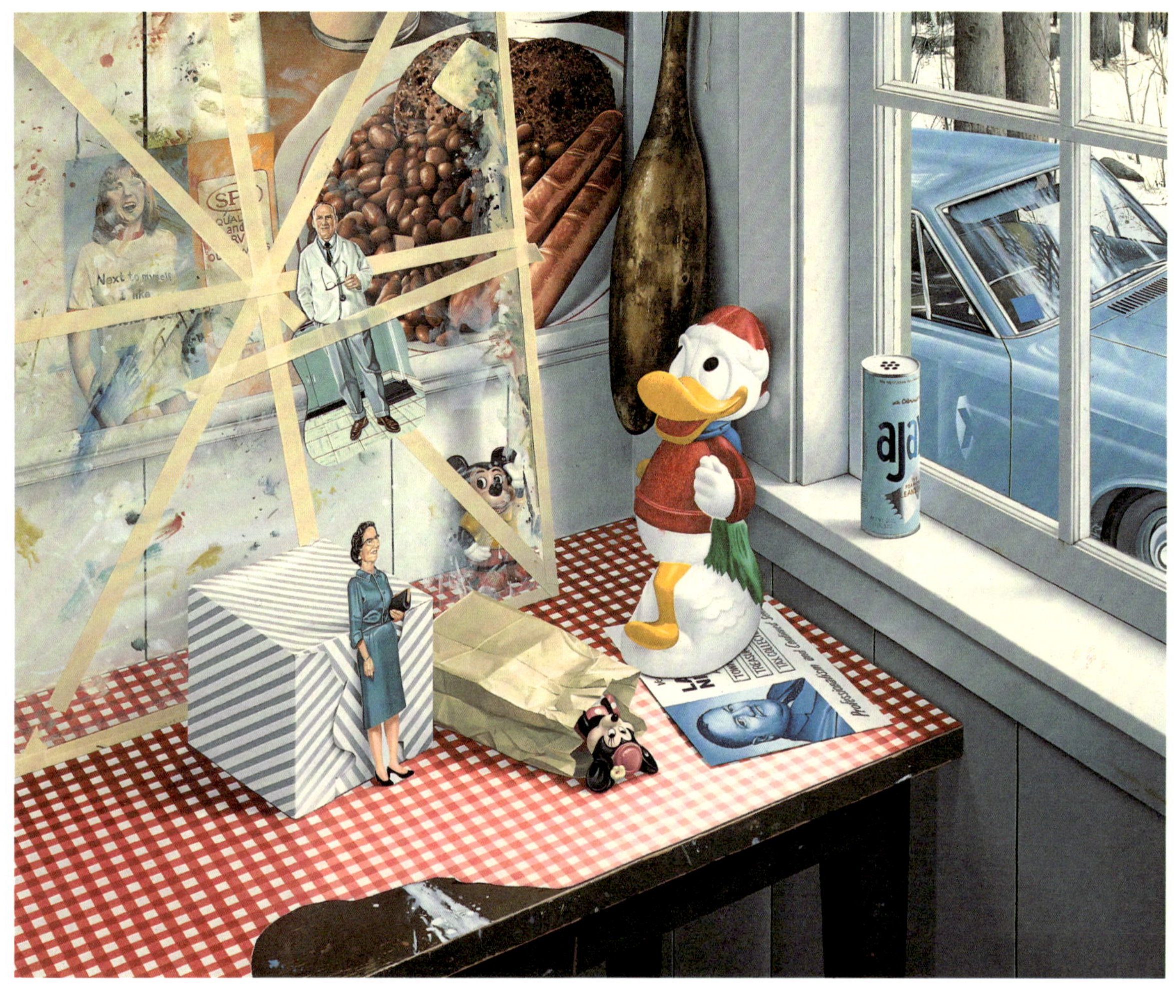

39

SCOTT PRIOR (b. 1949)

Christmas at MacDowell, 1979

Oil on masonite, 38 × 46

Rose Art Museum, Brandeis University, Waltham, Massachusetts;
Herbert W. Plimpton Collection

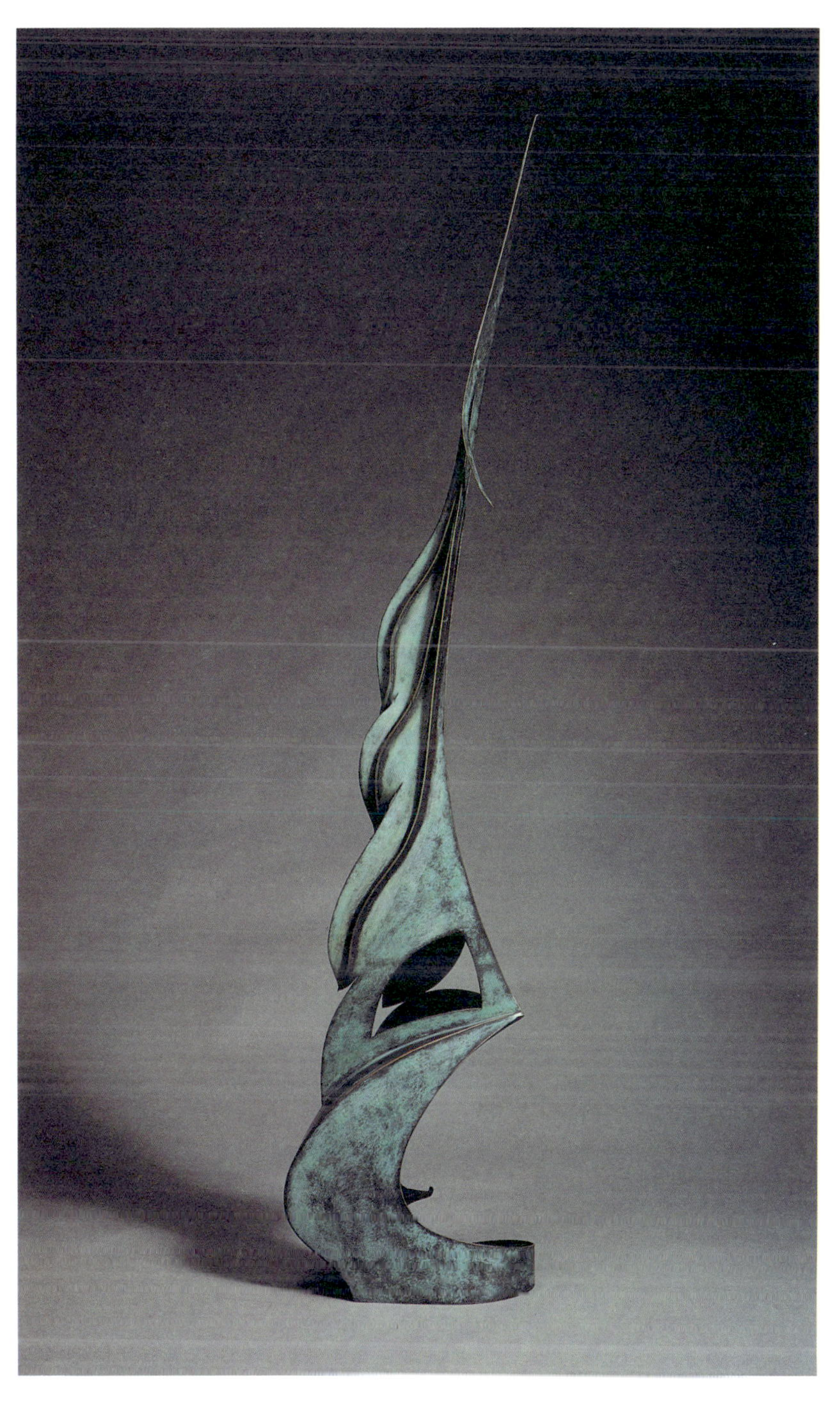

40
JOHN RAIMONDI (b. 1948)
Lupus, 1982
Bronze, 47 × 10 × 6
Collection of Ralph T. Cantin

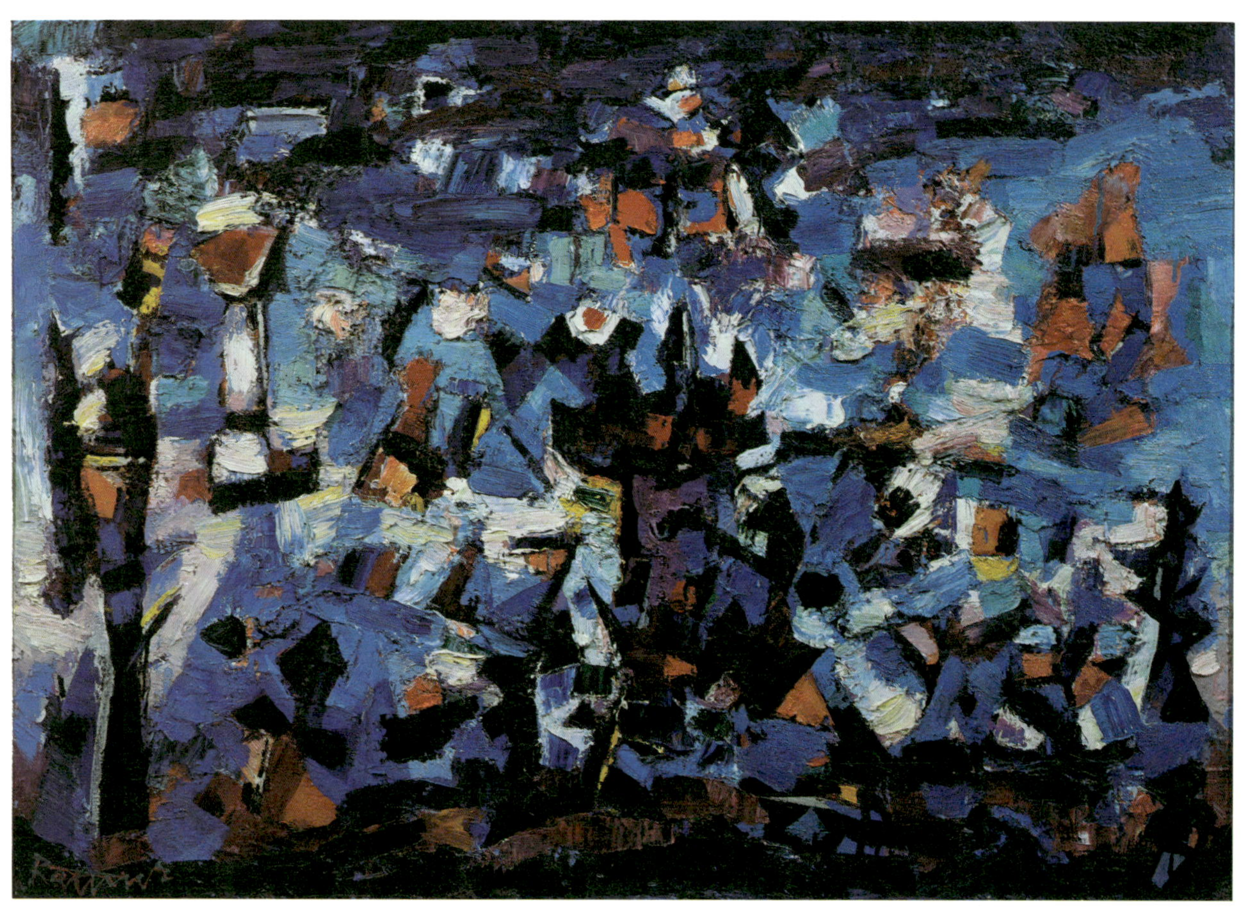

41

ABRAHAM RATTNER (1895–1978)
Storm Composition #3, 1955

Oil on panel, 27 × 37
Courtesy Kennedy Galleries Inc., New York

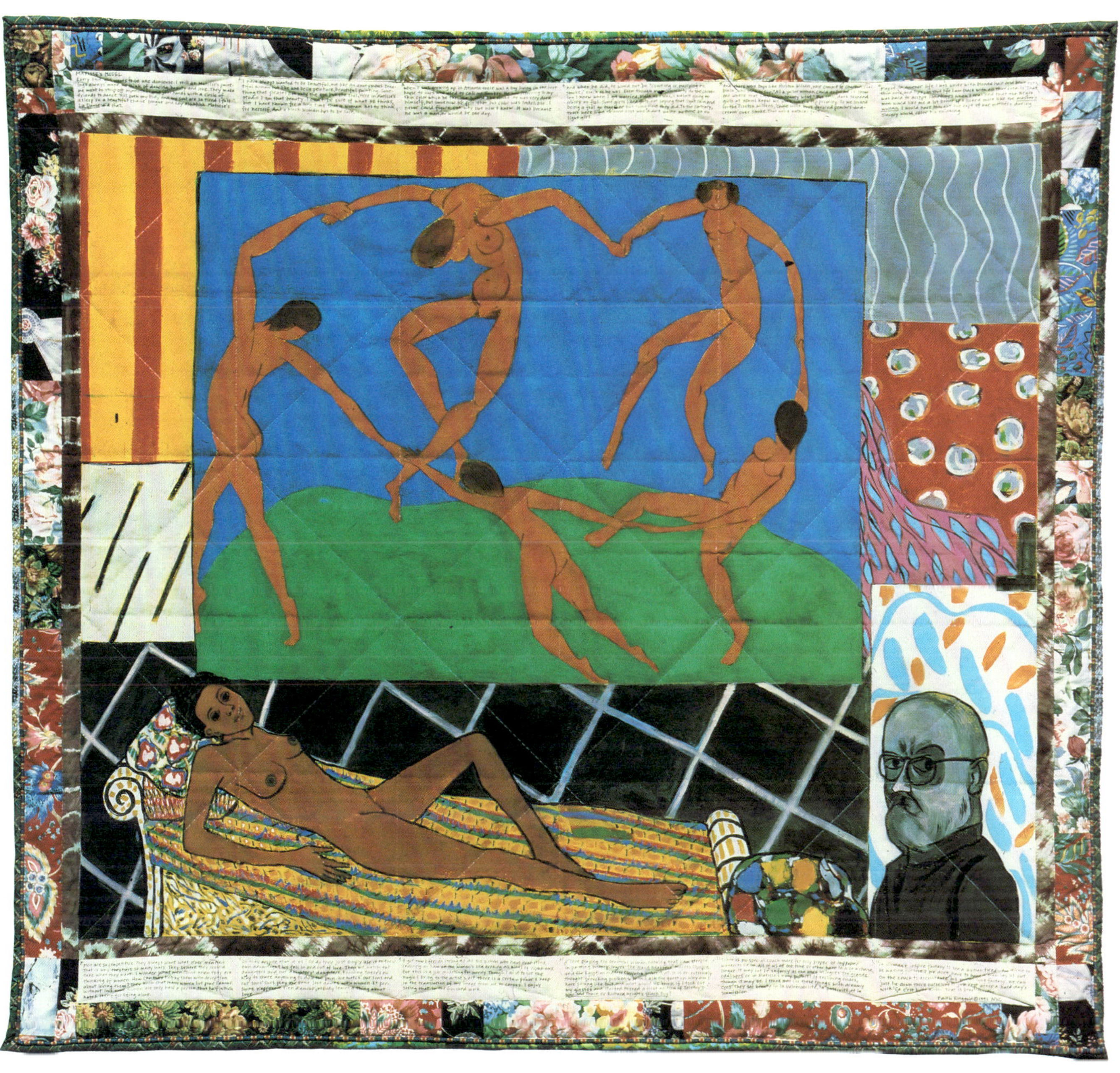

42

FAITH RINGGOLD (b. 1930)

The French Collection Part I: #5, Matisse's Model, 1991

Acrylic on canvas, pieced fabric border, 73½ × 79½

Courtesy ACA Galleries, New York / Munich

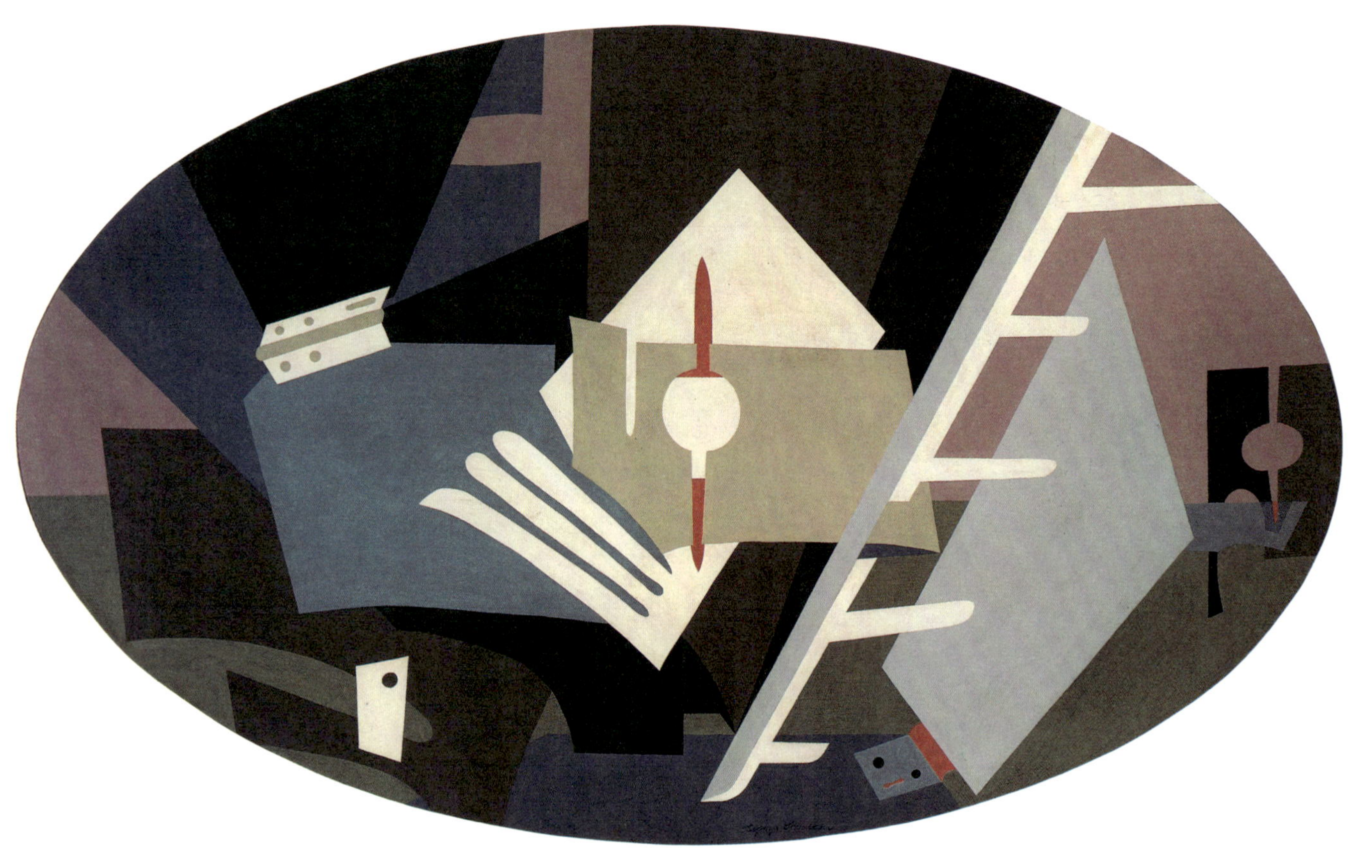

43
ESPHYR SLOBODKINA (b. 1908)
Composition in an Oval, about 1953
Oil on board, 32½ × 61½
Grey Art Gallery & Study Center, New York University Art Collection;
Gift of Mr. and Mrs. Irving Walsey, 1962

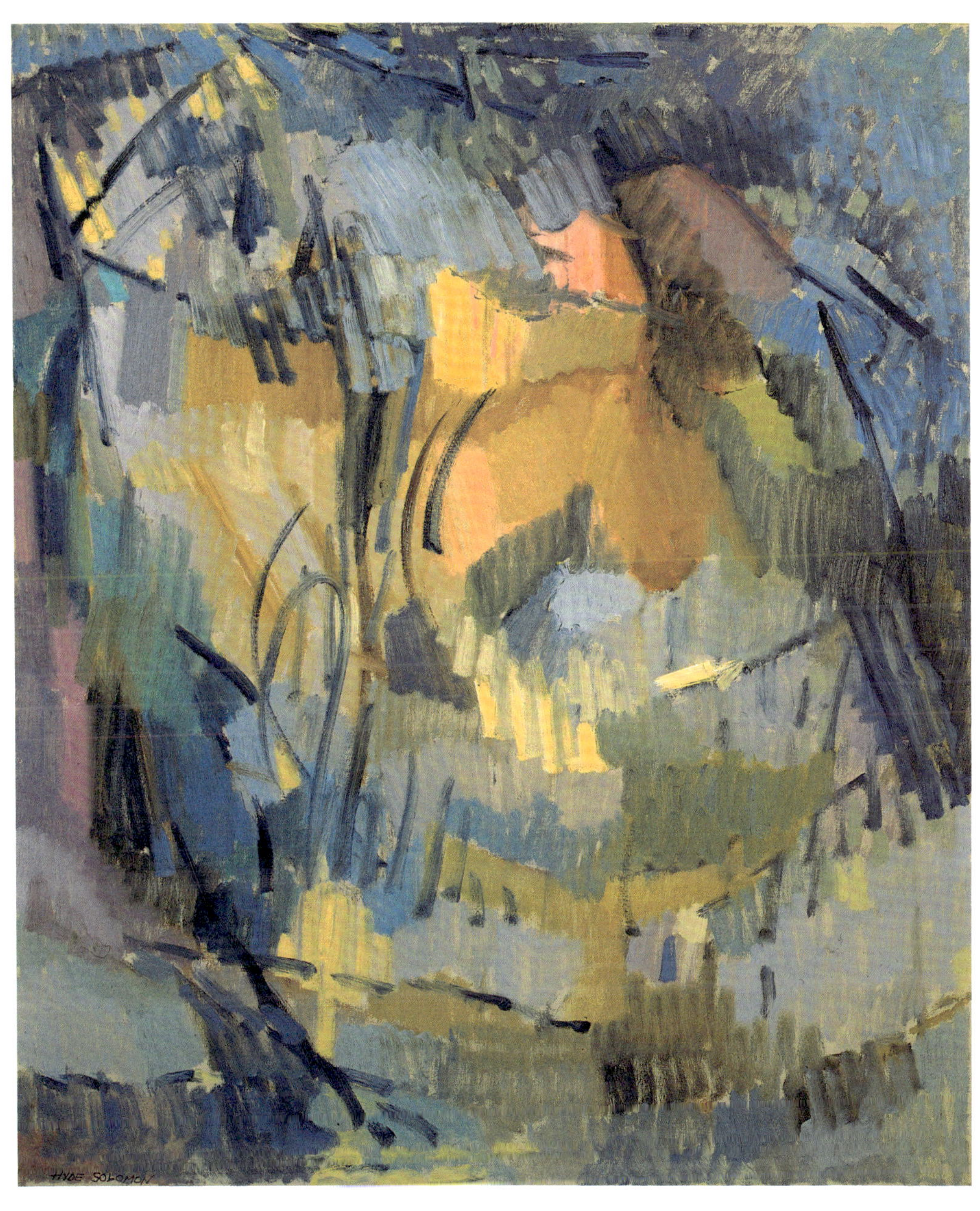

44
HYDE SOLOMON (b. 1911)
On the Way to the Islands, 1958
Oil on canvas, 57 × 48
Neuberger Museum of Art, Purchase College,
State University of New York; Gift of Roy R. Neuberger

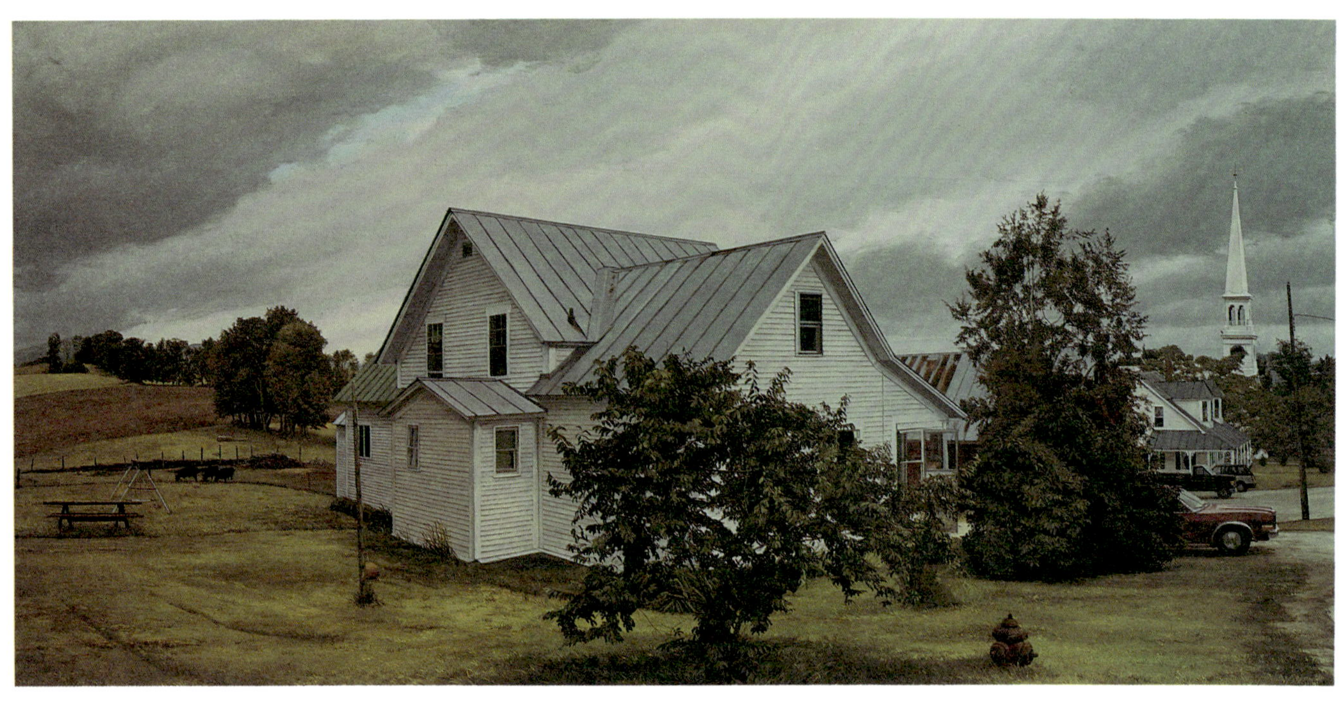

45
ALTOON SULTAN (b. 1948)
Village Street, Peacham, Vermont, 1989
Oil on canvas, 23¾ × 47¾
Courtesy Marlborough Gallery, Inc., New York

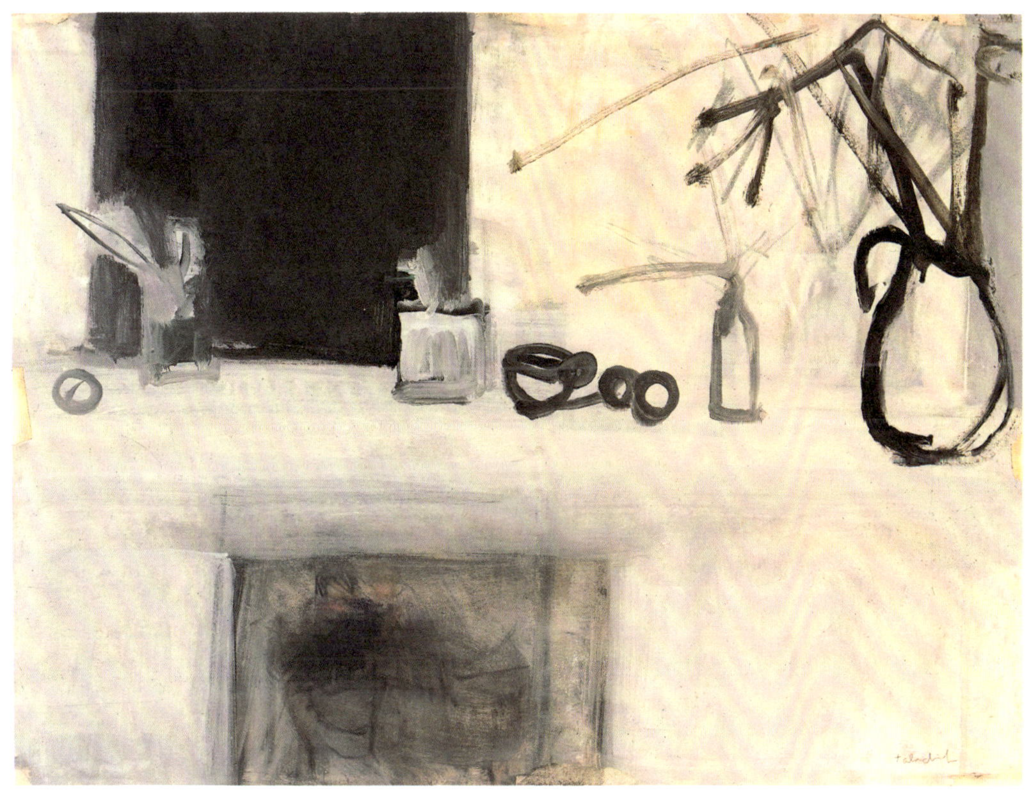

46
ANNE TABACHNICK (1927–1995)
Still Life, 1962
Mixed media on paper, 18 1/16 × 24
University Gallery, University of Massachusetts at Amherst

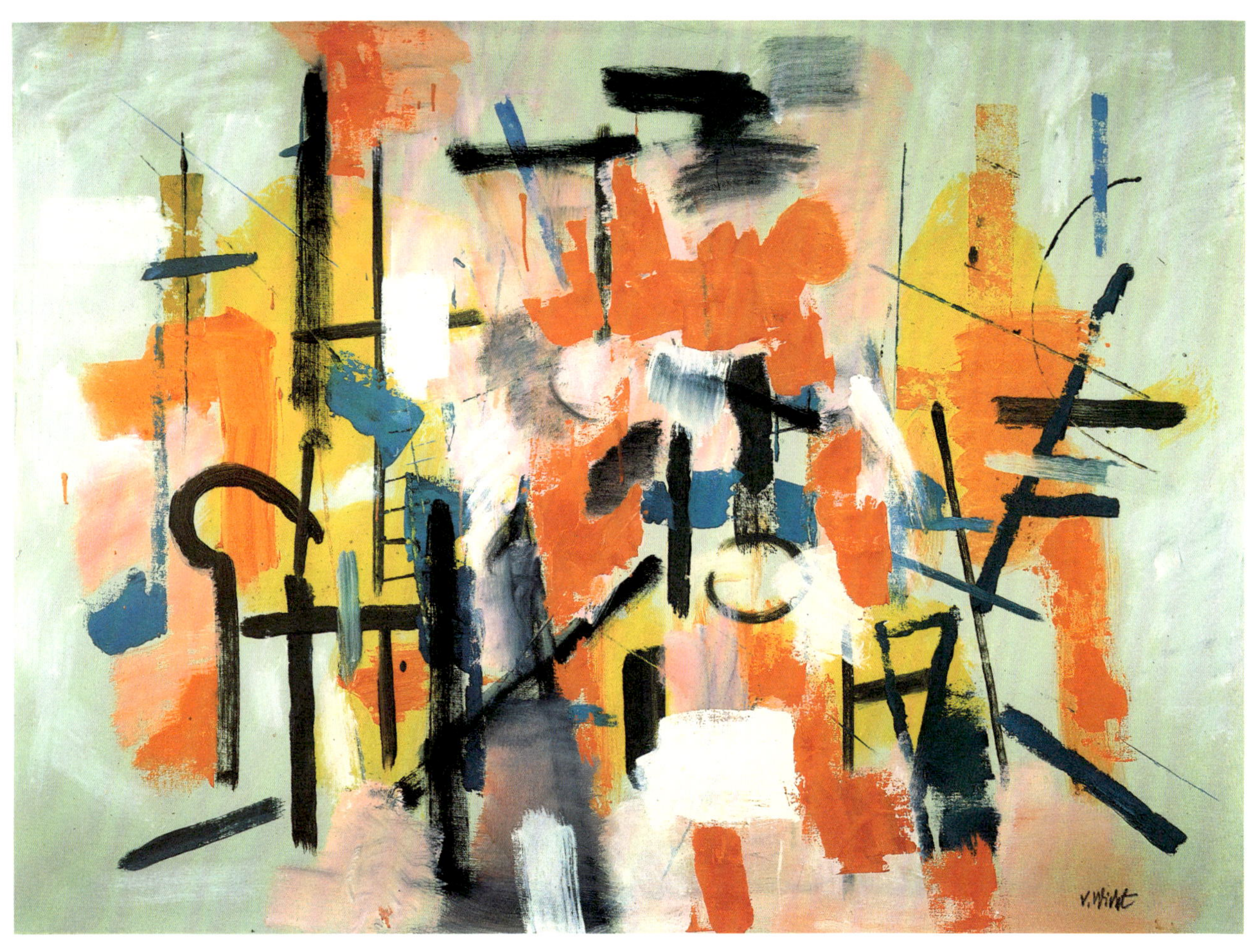

47

JOHN VON WICHT (1888–1970)

Harbor from Brooklyn Heights, 1957

Oil on canvas, 36 × 49

The Montclair Art Museum; Gift of Mr. and Mrs. Harvey Reisman

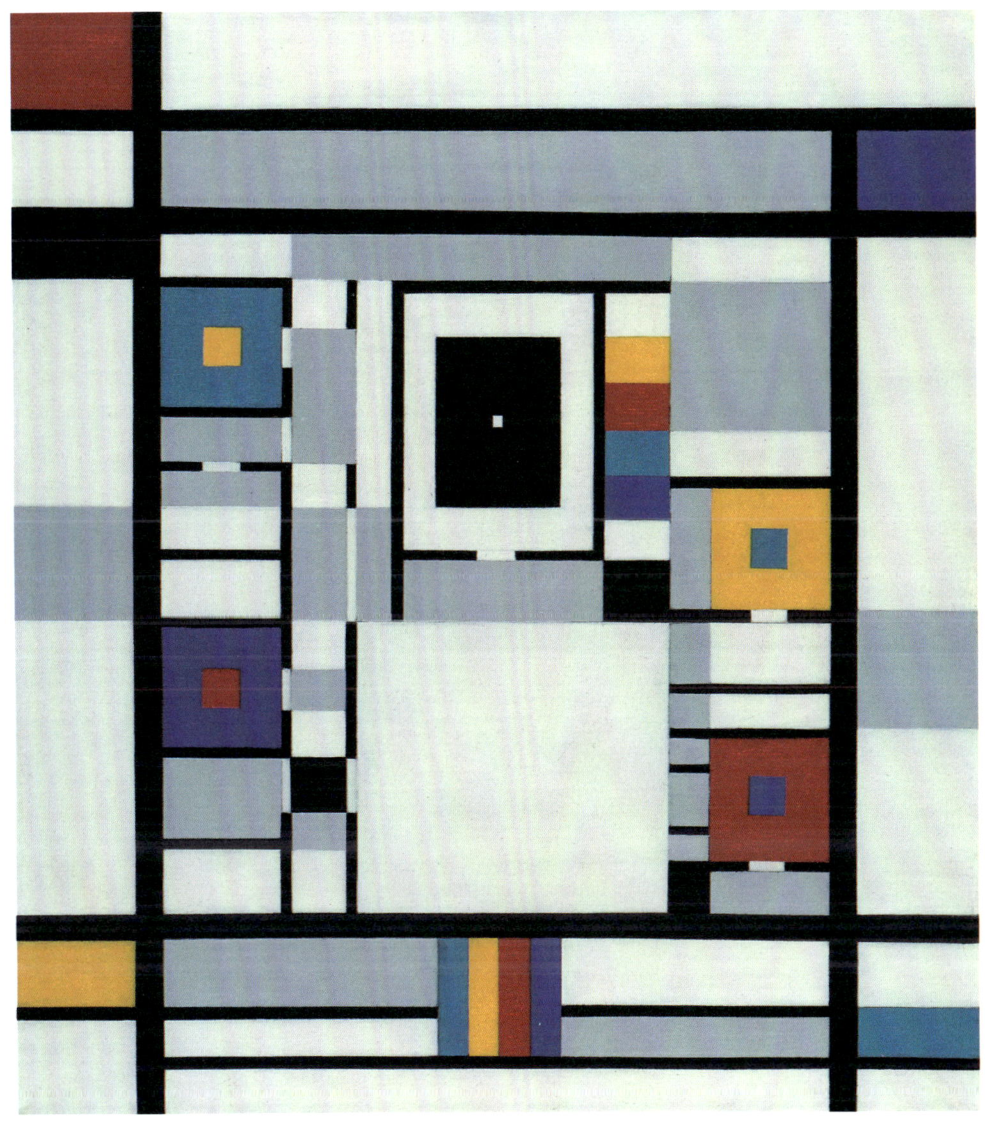

48
CHARMION VON WIEGAND (1899–1983)
Sanctuary of the Four Directions, 1959–60
Oil on canvas, 36 × 32
The Museum of Modern Art, New York;
The Riklis Collection of McCrory Corporation (fractional gift)

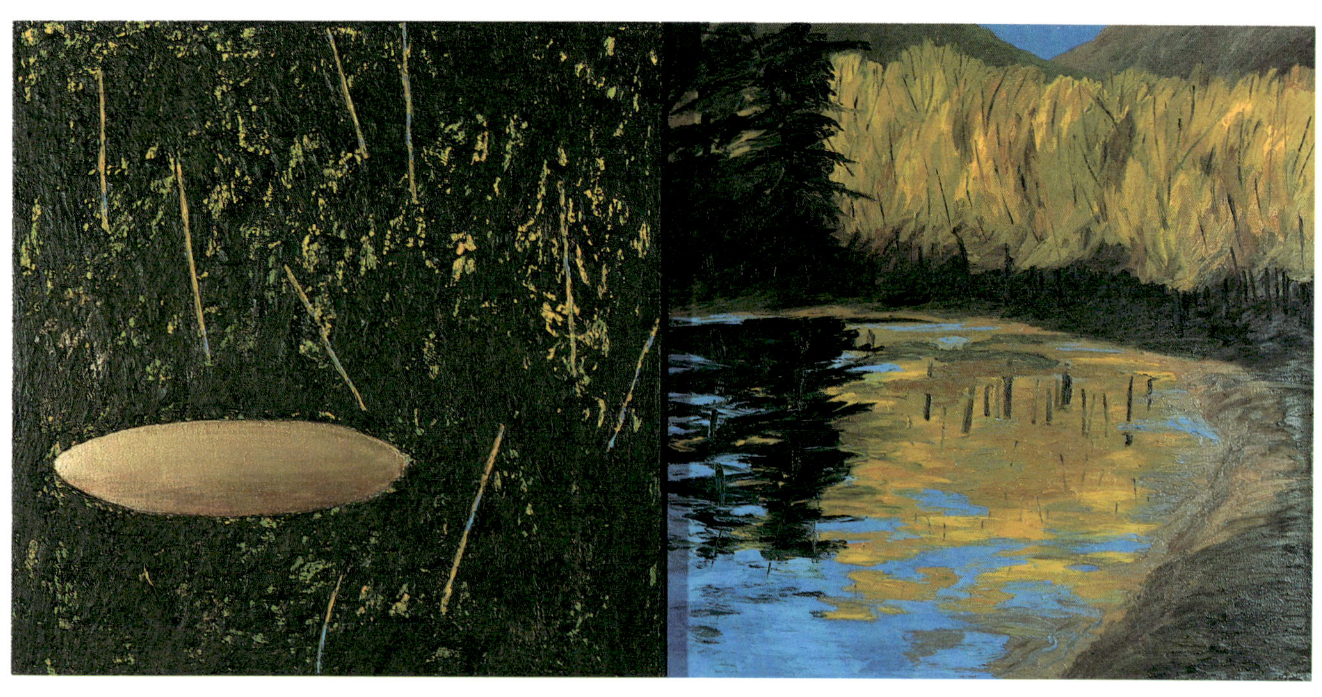

49
KAY WALKINGSTICK (b. 1935)
David's Pond, Var., 1987–95
Oil on canvas, 36 × 72
Collection of Michael David Echols

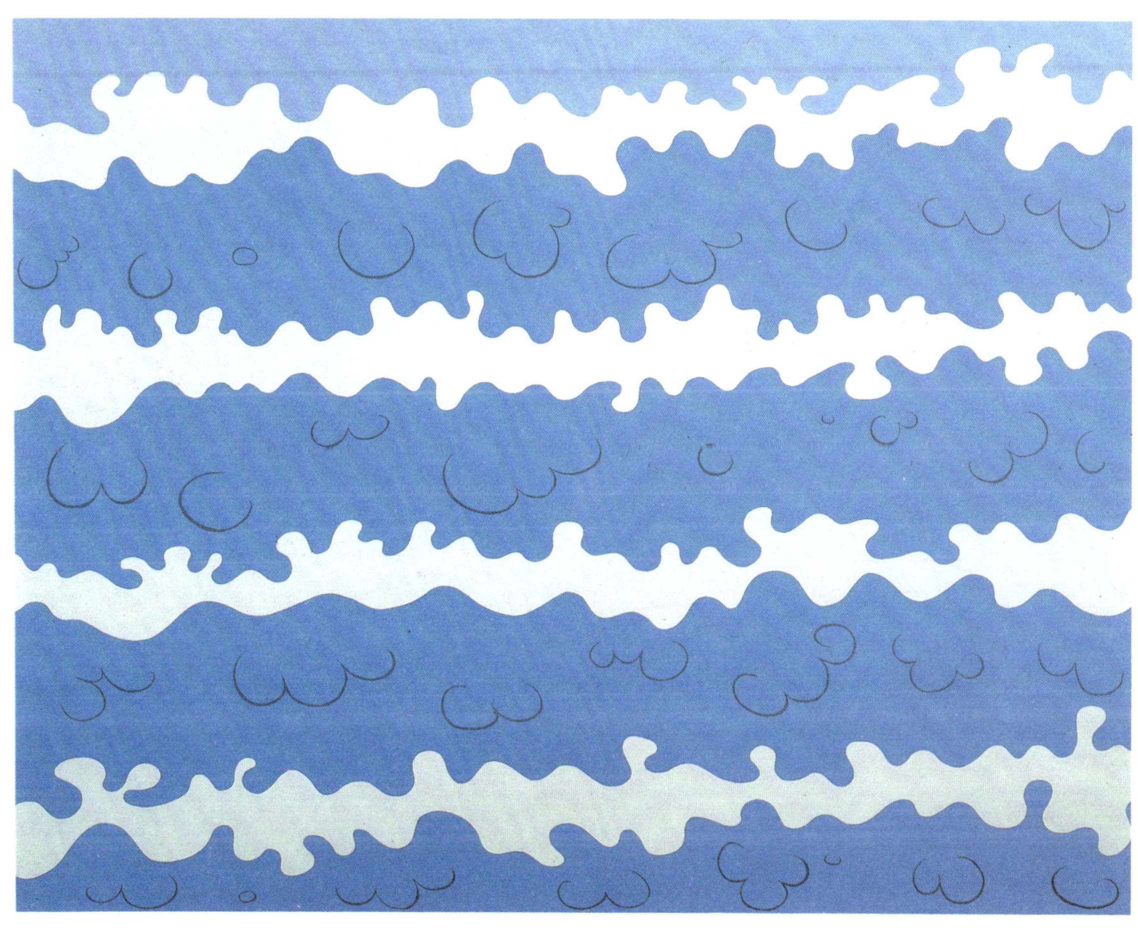

50
JOHN WESLEY (b. 1928)
Surf, 1978
Acrylic on canvas, 39 × 60
Courtesy Jessica Fredericks Gallery, New York

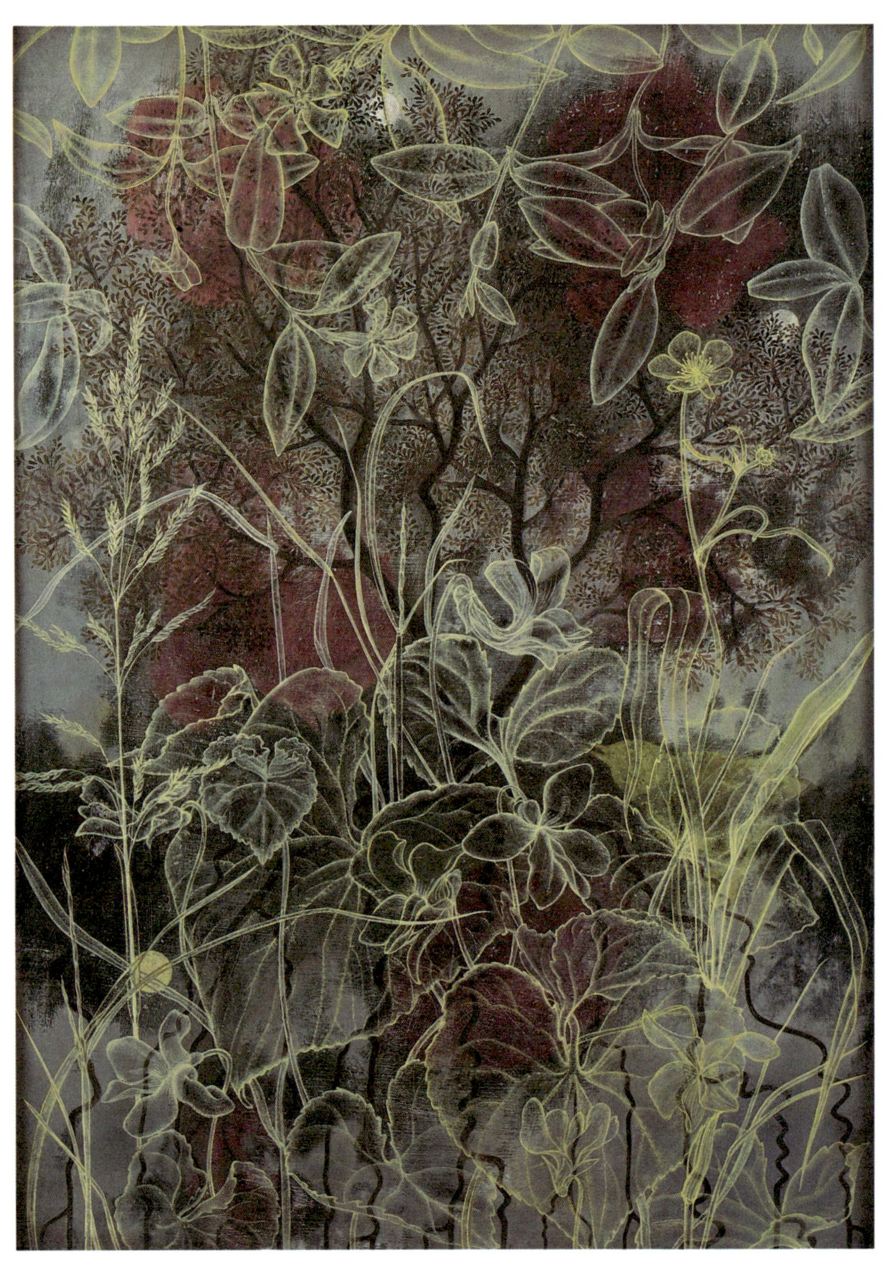

51
HELEN MIRANDA WILSON (b. 1948)
Season, 1991–95
Oil on panel, 14 × 10
Courtesy Jason McCoy, Inc., New York

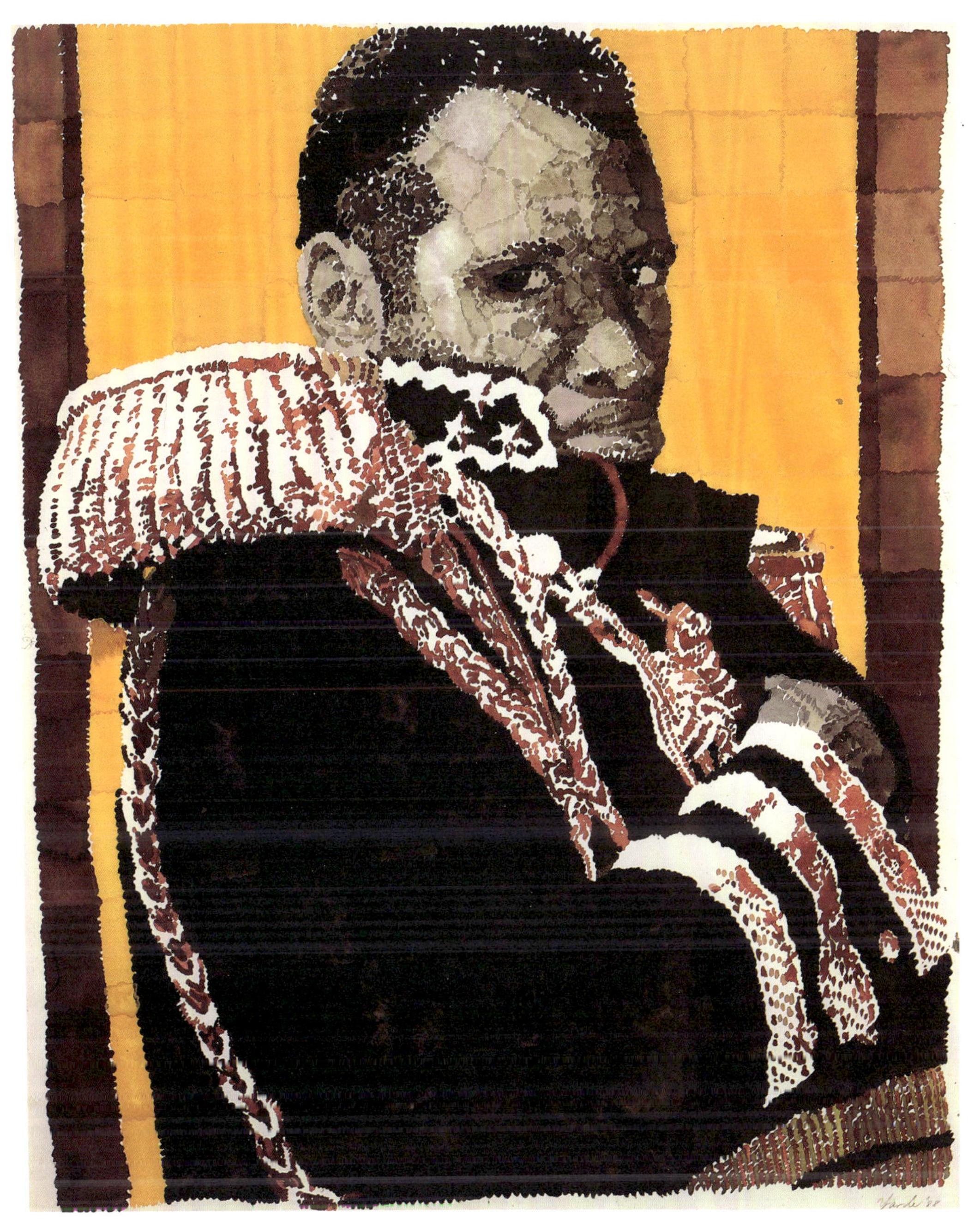

52

RICHARD YARDE (b. 1939)

Robeson as Emperor Jones, 1988

Watercolor, 41½ × 29½

Courtesy Wendell Street Gallery, Cambridge, Massachusetts

MacDowell Colony Fellows in Painting, Sculpture, and Drawing, with Their Years of Residency, 1908–1996

Abe, Kongo 1966, 67
Abel, Cora 1975, 77
Abramowicz, Janet 1975, 76
Abrams Collens, Vivien 1979, 81, 85
Abrams, Joyce 1985, 87
Acheson, Alice 1979
Acorn, John 1972
Adams, Alice 1966
Adams, Bill 1989
Adzema, Robert 1983
Agrons, Leonard 1968
Ahn, Dongkuk 1964
Ahrendt, Christine 1965, 66, 71
Ajar, Robert 1994–95
Alexander, Marsia 1974
Allen, Roberta 1971, 72, 73
Altman, Ellen 1972, 73, 74–75
Alvarez, Candida 1986
Andell, Nancy 1981
Anderson, Chris 1992
Anderson, Tennessee 1924, 25
Andrews, Benny 1973, 74, 75, 78
Antholt, Sharron 1984
Aono, Kristine Yuki 1990
Apfelbaum, Polly 1992, 93
Apostolides, Zoe 1979, 80
Arai, Tomie 1994
Asmar, Alice 1959, 60
Astrachan, Claude 1968
Atiyah, Donnette 1975
Attie, Dotty 1983
Avery, Milton 1953, 54, 56
Avery, Sally 1953, 54, 56
Awalt, Elizabeth 1982
Axelrod, Dee 1974, 76, 81–82
Bahc, Mo 1991
Bailey, Malcolm 1970
Baker, Ann 1979
Baker, Dina 1955
Baker, Mel 1980
Banks, Diane 1981
Baranik, Rudolf 1971, 72, 75, 77, 81, 82, 85–86, 87
Barbieri, Joseph 1969
Barchat, Meredith 1980
Barchers, Nelda 1977
Barjansky, Catharine 1946
Barnard, John 1969
Baroff, Jill 1988, 90
Barr, Virginia 1964
Bart, Harriet 1990
Bartlett, Kathy 1990
Bartoli, Jose 1975
Bassler, Lynn 1977
Batchelor, Betsey 1983
Bateman, Lisa 1982
Battle, Laura 1986
Baum, Louise 1973, 74
Bayer, Arlyne 1977
Beck, Margit 1957, 59, 60, 75
Beck, Rosemarie 1967, 70
Becker, Frederick 1923
Becker, Janice 1987
Bedgood, Jill 1988
Beerman, Herbert 1958, 59, 61, 67, 71–72
Beerman, Miriam 1959
Begheijn, Claire 1988
Behrens, Mary 1993, 94
Bel, Gladys 1989, 92
Belkin, Arnold 1974
Bell, Leland 1956, 57
Belloff, Mindy 1995
Beltzig, Stefan 1985
Belville, Scott 1979
Ben-Haim, Zigi 1990
Ben-Zion 1956, 58
Benitez-Stewart, Sylvia 1984, 85–86
Berger, Susan 1966, 67
Bergschneider, John 1953, 66
Berkowitz, Michael 1982, 86
Berlin, Daniel 1987
Berman, Phyllis 1985
Bermann, Lenora 1972
Berne, Betsy 1982–83, 89, 90
Bernstein, Ellen 1976
Berry, Inez 1960
Berry, William 1984
Bertoni, Christina 1991, 92, 93
Beube, Douglas 1986
Biddle, George 1956–57
Bien, Rene 1985
Binnie, Maureen 1985
Binning, Robin 1973, 74, 76
Bisbee, John 1995
Bishofs, Maris 1987
Blaine, Nell 1957
Blanke, Marie 1926
Blass, Charlotte 1935, 36, 37, 38, 48
Blavat, Mark 1985
Blum, Jerome 1934
Bohnenkamp, Leslie 1979
Bolger, Carole 1982
Bolotin, Jay 1975–76
Bono, Mary Joan 1973
Booher, Alvin 1963, 65, 68
Bordo, Robert 1994
Borgatta, Isabel 1968, 73, 74
Borgatta, Robert 1973, 74
Borowski, Wieslaw 1966, 70, 71
Bosley, Frederick 1919
Bowen, William 1952
Bozyan, Edith 1940, 41, 42
Brachman, Srule 1976
Bramlette, Teresa 1994

Branch, Kristina 1972
Brand, Ginna 1981, 83
Breger, Helen 1967
Brenson, Theodore 1959
Bressler, Martin 1964, 65, 73, 75
Brewster, Achsah 1908, 09, 10
Briggs, Ernest 1958
Brinley, D. Putnam 1921
Brock, Harry 1980, 84
Brodsky, Stan 1971
Brody, Lilly 1964, 67, 68, 72, 76
Broner, Mathew 1979
Brooks, James 1955
Brown, Linda 1984
Brown, Marvin 1970
Brown, Susan 1987
Brown, William 1969
Browne, Vivian 1980
Browning, Colleen 1956
Buchan, Virginia 1983
Buckley, Mary 1958
Buhler, Ken 1983
Buljeta, Ellen 1985
Bunch, Clarence 1966, 69
Burgess, James 1958, 61
Burke, Daniel 1970, 73
Burlin, Paul 1953, 54, 55, 57
Burns, Jerome 1964, 65, 67
Burns, Josephine 1960, 64, 65, 67
Burns, Maurice 1971–72, 74
Burpee, James 1976
Bush-Brown, Henry 1924
Bush-Brown, Lydia 1944
Bush-Brown, Margaret 1924
Bush, Clara 1967
Butler, Renee 1983
Byrne, Jacqueline 1971, 73
Byrne, Joseph 1985, 86
Caggiano, Margery 1968, 71
Cahill, Thomas 1995
Calcagno, Lawrence 1967, 68, 69, 70, 71, 72, 75, 76
Campanella, Vincent 1967
Campbell, David 1976
Campbell, Robin 1961
Candell, Victor 1949, 50, 51, 53
Canelake, Patricia 1995
Capaldi, Patti 1991
Capey, Katherine 1941, 42, 43, 44, 45, 46
Capey, Reco 1941, 42, 43, 44
Carlson, Cynthia 1976
Carmer, Elizabeth 1937, 38, 40, 41, 48
Carr, Sarah 1981
Carroll, Mary Ellen 1991
Carton, Norman 1961, 63
Castrucci, Andrew 1994
Catherwood, Beth 1986
Cavallon, Giorgio 1955
Cavanaugh, Thomas 1973–74
Cernuda, Paloma 1988–89
Chabot, Aurore 1991
Chadwick, Grace 1946
Chamberlin, F. Tolles 1913, 14, 15
Chan, Phillip 1980
Chandler, John 1974
Chaney, Ruth 1942
Chao, Bruce 1985
Chariot, Henri 1970–71
Charkow, Natalie 1965, 66, 67
Chase, Ben 1989
Chase, Ronald 1958, 59, 60–61, 62–63, 64, 65
Chelminski, Michael 1967
Cheng, Amy 1989, 92
Chiesa, Wilfredo 1979
Chiros, Jim 1985–86, 89
Chisman, Dale 1975
Chiu, Ten 1957, 58
Ciarrochi, Ray 1962, 65
Ciarrochi, Sandra 1965
Ciesluk, Karl 1993
Citron, Minna 1955, 57
Clapp, Marcia 1931, 32
Clark, Ursula 1994
Clay, Willy 1978
Cloonan, Aileen 1965
Clyne, Maureen 1984
Coates, Jim 1988
Cobble, Brian 1978–79, 80–81
Coburn, Cynthia 1984–85, 89
Cochran, Michael 1988
Cockcroft, Eva 1986
Coen, Nadia 1994
Cohen-Edelman, Gail 1987
Cohen, George 1958
Cohen, Nancy 1981, 86
Cohen, Rachel 1965, 66, 68
Colarusso, Corrinne 1977, 79
Coleman, Glenn 1917
Collery, Paula 1984, 85
Colton, Maurice 1978
Conde, Miguel 1966
Connah, Ferris 1921
Conover, Robert 1955, 56, 57, 58
Cooke, Alvin 1963
Cooper, Ann 1992
Cooper, Barbara 1991
Cooper, Paul 1976
Corbett, Edward 1966
Costigan, Constance 1977
Cottingham, Robert 1993, 94
Cottrell, Marsha 1994
Couture, Christin 1980
Cowdrick, Norma 1993
Cowles, Russell 1956
Cozza, Vincent 1979
Crane, Gregory 1982, 84
Craner, Robert 1970
Cravens, Curtis 1993
Crawford, Jane 1955
Crile, Susan 1972
Cross, Rebecca 1993
Culhane, Douglas 1987
Cullen, Catherine 1990
Cuming, Beatrice 1934, 38, 43, 44, 46, 52
Cunningham, Jan 1983
Cuppaidge, Virginia 1975
Curry-Cloonan, Aileen 1966, 69
Curtis, Lynn 1992
Curtis, Timothy 1983
Cushing, Barbara 1977, 81
Cyr, Annette 1992
Cyril, Ruth 1973–74
Czoka, Stephen 1947
D'Amario, Julia 1989
D'Arrigo, Elisa 1986, 87
D'Orazio, Jon 1973
Daborn, Erica 1984
Dahill, Thomas 1958
Dallos, Miklos 1963
Damato, Anthony 1961
Daniels, Eleanor 1985
Davidek, Gregory 1993
Davis, Stephen 1985
Day, John 1960, 61, 62, 64
Day, Larry 1978
Day, Linda 1987
Day, Worden 1940, 55, 56, 58, 63, 81
Daykin, Susan 1982
De St.Croix, Blane 1982
DeCaro, Pat 1982, 94
DeLuccia, Alyssa 1991
DeMoulpied, Deborah 1968–69, 70
DeNiro, Robert 1970
DeRocco, Jovan 1931, 32
Dean, Mark 1980
Decker, Elisa 1985
Decker, Greg 1992, 93
Deem, George 1977–78, 79
Dehn, Virginia 1971
Delgado Guitart, Jose 1973, 74
Dell, Robert 1980
Della-Volpe, Ralph 1963
Denghausen, Franz 1947
Denzinger, Katharina 1984, 85, 86
Derrickson, Steve 1991
Deshaies, Arthur 1959, 60, 61, 62
Devaney, John 1993
DiCapua, Ralph 1988, 90
DiLeo, Nicholas 1992
DiMatteo, Robert 1992
DiPietro, David 1991
Dickerson, Arthur 1959, 60, 61, 62
Dickerson, Daniel 1953
Dickinson, Nancy 1975
Diehl, Carol 1995
Dienes, Sari 1951, 53, 54
Dineen, Tom 1976, 77, 78
Dinhofer, Lisa 1983
Dinnerstein, Simon 1969, 79
Dintenfass, Marylyn 1988, 90
Djeneef, Ivan 1929, 30, 31
Dobbins, Anne 1965
Dodd, Kate 1991
Doe, Don 1985
Dolan, Janice 1973
Dombek, Blanche 1957, 66, 68, 69, 76
Donneson, Seena 1963, 64
Doran, Matt 1954
Doubrava, Jan 1964, 65, 66
Dougherty, Devin 1987
Dougherty, Maureen 1981–82
Douglas, Laura 1948
Downs, Cile 1977
Drabkin, Catherine 1991
Draney, Sarah 1978, 81
Drasher, Kathy 1990
Drescher, Karl 1973
Drexler, Sherman 1964
Driscoll, Ellen 1983
Drumheller, Grant 1982
Dubin, Ralph 1976
Dubinskis, Anda 1987
Dunkelman, Loretta 1981
Duval, Barbara 1985
Duval, Jeanne 1981, 83, 93
Eastman, Louise 1994
Edelstein, Barbara 1991
Edwards, Beth 1994
Edwards, Ethel 1957
Edwards, Wendy 1978
Eklind, Marjorie 1979
Eldredge, Letitia 1976
Elias, Arthur 1977
Elliott, Dennis 1971
Elliott, Ronnie 1956
Ellis, Dean 1956
Ellison, Victoria 1988–89, 90
Elman, Emily 1969, 73
Elton, Lynne 1981
Emanuel, Martin 1989
Emerson, Sybil 1935
Emmart, Dale 1986
Engelson, Carol 1967, 71, 72–73, 74

Keizer, Susan 1986
Keller, Carol 1987
Keller, Martha 1989, 90
Kelley, Donald 1966, 68, 73
Kelly, Robert 1980
Kendall, Beatrice 1933
Kendrick, Barbara 1993
Kennedy, Brigid 1983, 85
Kerlin, Sherry 1992
Kerrigan, Maurie 1985–86, 86–87
Kersh, Nora 1964, 65
Kevles, Dina 1959
Kezur, David 1989, 90
Kihlstedt, Maja 1981
Kilbourn, Victoria 1966, 68
Kilmartin, Christopher 1985
Kimura, Hiroshi 1996
King, John S. 1983
King, William 1977
Kirby, Glo 1957
Kirschenbaum, Jules 1969
Kitman, Suzy 1993
Kitzmiller, Carol 1955
Klein, Barbara 1989
Klement Shapey, Vera 1957, 58, 59
Klemperer, Wendy 1986
Klimowicz, Henry 1986
Klitgaard, Georgina 1965, 66
Klix, Richard 1958, 60
Knight, Dusty 1985
Koczy, Rosemarie 1980, 81
Koenig, Peter 1964
Koffman, Nathan 1948
Komatsu, Fumi 1962, 63, 64
Kometani, Foumiko 1960, 61
Korman, Gerald 1971
Kory, Genevieve 1956
Kowal, Dennis 1965, 72
Kowalok, Patricia 1980, 81
Kozlow, Sigmund 1948
Kraft, Arthur 1947
Krauss, Anthony 1964, 65, 66, 67, 68
Kreymborg, Dorothy 1923, 33, 41, 45, 50, 51
Kriesberg, Irving 1970, 75, 77, 78, 79, 82
Kruse-Sokoloff, Melinda 1976, 77, 79, 80
Kunzler, Frederic 1964
Kurz, Diana 1977
LaFond, Louise 1984–85
LaRoche, Charles 1962, 76
Laguna, Muriel 1965, 69, 73, 75, 76
Lam, Jennett 1960, 61
Lane, Bent 1957
Lang, Daniel 1967, 68
Lansford, Gretchen 1955
Larsen, Mernet 1966
Lasker, Joe 1967
Lavanoux, Maurice 1921
Lawless, Sharon 1990
Lawley, Elizabeth 1983
Learner, Martha 1973–74
Lee, Lanie 1987
Leigh, Harry 1968, 69, 70, 72, 74, 75, 83, 85, 86
Lenski, Willy 1987, 91
Leon, Alan 1981
Leon, Dennis 1981
Leonardi, Hector 1964
Leopold, Susan 1994, 95
Lerman, Ora 1977
Lerner, Marilyn 1989
Letven, Wendy 1993
Levey, Jeffrey 1930, 31, 32, 33, 34, 35, 38, 41, 44
Levine, Arnold 1976
Levitan, Idee 1956
Levitan, Israel 1956
Levitt, Alfred 1956
Levitt, William 1976
Levy, Ann 1987
Lewis, Harold 1958, 62–63
Lewis, Jeffrey 1987
Lewis, Phillip 1985
Lide, Elizabeth 1982
Lieberman, Louis 1983
Ligon, Glenn 1989
Lin, Cynthia 1994
Lindberg, Linda 1955
Lindell, John 1992
Linden, Carl 1931
Lindquist, Mark 1979
Link, B. Lillian 1913, 14, 19
Linn, Steve 1980
Lins, Pamela 1988
Lipfert, Theo 1992
Lipkin, Lawrence 1993
Lipton, Jackie 1988
Lishinsky, Saul 1948, 58
Lisieski, Peter 1979
Lithgow, Kenneth 1968
Livingston, Sidnee 1960, 63
Lloyd, Marcia 1980
Lo, William 1979
Loftus, Ryan 1992
Long, Jeff 1987
Lorence, John 1962, 63, 64, 65
Lorenz, Elaine 1981
Loye, Kate 1991
Lucas, Craig 1983
Ludwig, Daniel 1993–94
Lum, Mary 1994
Lyndon, Andrew 1991
Maakestad, Susan 1994
MacAlister, Helen 1995–96
MacFarlane, Stewart 1978
MacKendrick, Lilian 1975
MacNea, Edith 1913, 14
MacPhee, Medrie 1980
Maguire, Anna 1968
Maguire, Douglas 1968
Main, Tim 1988, 90, 94
Malmborg, Britt 1979
Malone, Lois 1978, 82
Mangione, Patricia 1957, 58, 59, 60, 64, 67, 71, 74, 75
Manning, William 1965
Mantooth, Henrietta 1990
Marcus, Marcia 1969
Margo, Boris 1955
Margolis, Margo 1976
Marin, Manuel 1986
Marlow, Shelley 1992
Marquart, Allegra 1991
Marsen, Roxi 1984
Marshall, Mona 1975, 76, 83
Martin, Helen 1942, 45
Martin, Josie 1995
Martin, Paul 1986
Martin, Rebecca 1994
Martinez, Ricardo 1963–64
Martino, Babette 1983
Marx, Nicki 1975
Mason, Alice 1967
Mattiasdottir, Louisa 1956, 57
Mayer, Bena 1960, 61
Mayer, Ralph 1960, 61
Mayer, Sondra 1978
Mayhew, Richard 1958
Maynard, Valerie 1991–92
McBride, Margaret 1984
McCabe, Maureen 1988
McCabe, Sigrid 1986
McCoubrey, Sarah 1990
McDonald, Edward 1986
McDonnell, Henry 1966, 68
McDonnell, Mary 1991
McGee, Carrie 1989–90
McIntosh, David 1966–67
McIntyre, Lynda 1980
McKean, Hugh 1937
McNamara, John 1985
McNichol, Jane 1985
Mears, Helen 1908, 09, 10, 11
Mendelsohn, Vera 1966
Merz, Katie 1995
Metz, Kathryn 1966, 67
Meyer, Henry 1969
Mikus, Eleanore 1969
Miles, Jeanne 1966
Milholland, Richard 1974, 75
Miller, Jane 1989, 92
Miller, Mark 1992, 93
Miller, R. Guy 1968
Mills, Thomas 1992
Mim, Adrienne 1972, 73, 74
Minich, Anne 1984, 88, 89
Mitchell, Garry 1982
Mitchell, Tyrone 1968
Mitrevics, Maximilian 1956
Miyashita, Tad 1972, 73, 74
Mochizawa, Osamu 1992
Mommer, Paul 1938
Monaghan, Gertrude 1918
Monroe, Gerald 1973, 76
Monti, John 1987
Mooney, John 1972, 73, 87, 90
Moore, Claire 1945, 77, 79
Moore, David 1984, 86
Moore, Marjorie 1989
Moore, Mary 1961
Morera, Gabriel 1963, 64, 65
Morgan, Robert 1990
Morris, George 1969, 70, 73
Morris, Gregg 1978–79
Morrison, Holly 1991
Moses, Richard 1967
Moss, Ben 1992
Mulvey, Steven 1989
Mumford, Mark 1988–89
Munson, Portia 1992
Murphy, Margaret 1993
Murway, Dorothy 1972
Myrick, Burney 1953
Nadel, Barbara 1966–67
Naiman, Jon 1991
Nash, Mary 1977
Nathan, Piotr 1995
Neagoe, Anna 1950, 51
Newman, Bonnie 1987
Newman, John 1993
Newman, Laura 1984
Nguyen, Quang 1993
Nichter, Susan 1984
Niemeier, William 1996
Niemeyer, John 1917
Noble, Diane 1990
Nordhausen, A. 1933, 34, 37
O'Connor, Charles 1975
O'Reilly, Geraldine 1991
Olds, Elizabeth 1957, 65
Olmstead, Westley 1972
Ortbal, Robert 1994
Ortner, Frederick 1975
Osborne, Elizabeth 1983
Osgood, Christopher 1989–90
Osip, Sandra 1992
Ossoff, Deborah 1981, 86
Otto, Waldemar 1995
Overbay, Paula 1991, 94
Paeff, Bashka 1916, 17, 19, 21,

Community of Creativity
A Century of MacDowell Colony Artists
was designed by
Gilbert Design Associates
and printed by
Meridian Printing in Rhode Island.

✦

The paper is Monadnock Dulcet text and cover,
an acid free stock
produced in New Hampshire
by Monadnock Paper Mills.

✦

The typeface is Fournier,
cut for Monotype in 1924.
The design is named after and based on the work of
the eighteenth-century French designer
Pierre-Simon Fournier.

✦

The book was bound by the Riverside Group
in New York.

✦

2,500 copies on the occasion of the exhibition
at The Currier Gallery of Art,
September
1996.